Key Stage 3 Maths is a complete revision package. It comprises clear, concise content, covering everything in the programme of study for this Key Stage, plus tasks and questions to reinforce pupils' learning and help improve their confidence. As such, it provides a user-friendly and cost-effective alternative to traditional revision guides with separate workbooks.

This book is intended for pupils who will be sitting the Tier 3-5 and Tier 4-6 papers in the National Curriculum Mathematics Tests at the end of Year 9. It is meticulously matched to the programme of study for Key Stage 3 and the material is organised into different levels, according to the attainment targets set out in the National Curriculum.

For easy reference, the pages are colour-coded according to level. Material for **Levels 3 and 4** can be found on the **red** pages. Material for **Levels 5 and 6** can be found on the **blue** pages.

The book is arranged into four sections: Number; Algebra; Shape, Space & Measure; and Handling Data. Each section is broken down into topics. Within each topic, the **Level 5 and 6 (blue)** material follows on immediately from the **Level 3 and 4 (red)** material to provide obvious progression. All pupils, regardless of ability, should revise the **Level 3 and 4 (red)** pages as they provide an essential platform to the higher material.

Each page starts with bullet points identifying exactly what the pupil needs to know. It then provides clear explanations with easy-to-follow, worked examples followed by questions for the pupil to complete, ensuring they can use the different skills to solve problems accurately.

Consultant Editor: John Proctor
An Education Consultant with over 13 years' teaching experience, John Proctor is an expert in Mathematics and Computer Science. He is the former Director of Specialist College, St. Mary's Catholic High School in Astley.

Contributors:

Linda Bakes
Linda Bakes has over 21 years' experience teaching mathematics. She has also lectured in the subject at Leeds Metropolitan University and worked as a Mathematics Consultant to West Yorkshire Education Business Services.

Susan Ball
As a marker for National Curriculum Tests in Mathematics, Susan Ball knows better than most where pupils struggle and make mistakes. An experienced teacher and lecturer, she is an established maths author with several Key Stage 3 text books and teachers' resources in print.

... Browse for a full list of publications and further information

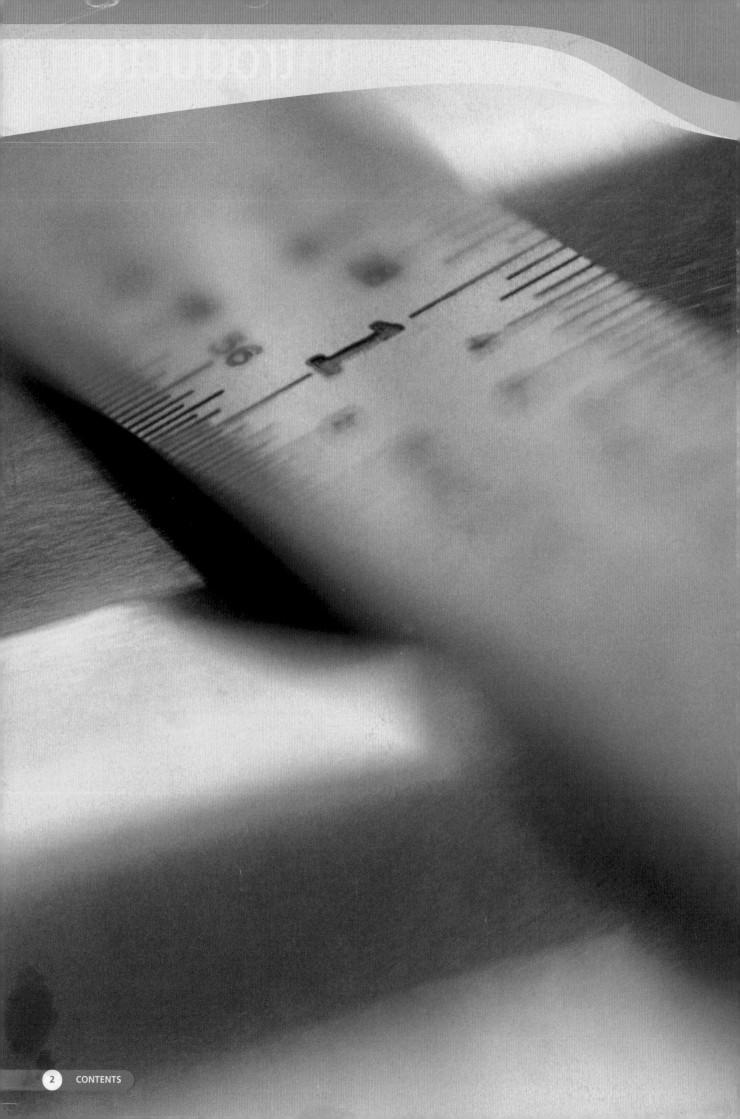

Contents

You need to know...

- **the place value of digits in numbers up to 1000**
- **how to arrange numbers in order of size.**

The value of a digit in a whole number depends on its position in the number. A digit can represent units, tens, hundreds, thousands, etc. The place values can be extended for larger numbers such as ten thousands, hundred thousands, millions and beyond as required. This is what a place value table looks like…

Place Value of Digits				Number
1000 Thousands	**100** Hundreds	**10** Tens	**1** Units	
		2	7	Twenty seven
	6	5	9	Six hundred and fifty nine
3	1	8	5	Three thousand, one hundred and eighty five

Place value can help you to arrange numbers in order of size, from smallest to largest (ascending order) or from largest to smallest (descending order).

For example, take the numbers 1786, 546, 4268 and 321. If you put the numbers in a place value table it is easy to see which is biggest:

Place Value of Digits			
1000 Thousands	**100** Hundreds	**10** Tens	**1** Units
1	7	8	6
	5	4	6
4	2	6	8
	3	2	1

Look at the digits in the thousands column first. 4 is bigger than 1, so 4268 is bigger than 1786.

Now look at the hundreds. 5 is bigger than 3, so 546 is bigger than 321.

So, in descending order the numbers are: 4268, 1786, 546, 321.

Now try these...

1. Draw a place value table like the one at the top of the page. Put the following numbers into it as digits and words:
   a) thirty four
   b) one hundred and seventy nine
   c) six hundred and three
   d) seven thousand, four hundred and two
   e) nine thousand, nine hundred and eighty nine
   f) six thousand and twelve
   g) 107
   h) 44 (watch the spelling!)
   i) 5423
   j) 777
   k) 1011

2. Put the following numbers into descending order:
   75, 80, 37, 73, 101

3. Put the following numbers into ascending order:
   321, 765, 568, 300, 876

Place Value

You need to know...

- **how to use the place value table to help you multiply and divide by 10, 100 or 1000.**

In a place value table, each column to the left is 10 times bigger than the previous one. This provides a quick method for multiplying and dividing by 10, 100, 1000…

Example

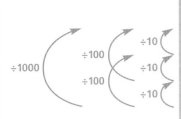

1000 Thousands	100 Hundreds	10 Tens	1 Units
			7
		7	0
	7	0	0
7	0	0	0

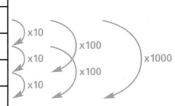

So

$7 \times 10 = 70$

$7 \times 100 = 700$ ⟶ $70 \times 10 = 700$

$7 \times 1000 = 7000$ ⟶ $70 \times 100 = 7000$ ⟶ $700 \times 10 = 7000$

And

$7000 \div 1000 = 7$ ⟶ $700 \div 100 = 7$ ⟶ $70 \div 10 = 7$

$7000 \div 100 = 70$ ⟶ $700 \div 10 = 70$

$7000 \div 10 = 700$

? Now try these...

Copy and complete these statements:

1. a) $8 \times 100 = $ ....
   b) $80 \times 100 = $ ....
   c) $800 \times $ .... $= 8000$

2. a) $9 \times $ .... $= 900$
   b) $9000 \div 100 = $ ....
   c) $90 \div $ .... $= 9$

3. a) $56 \times 10 = $ ....
   b) $560 \times 10 = $ ....
   c) $5600 \div 100 = $ ....

4. a) $8100 \div 10 = $ ....
   b) $81 \times 100 = $ ....
   c) $810 \div $ .... $= 81$

ⓘ You need to know...

- **how to recognise negative numbers.**

When counting objects we usually start at 0 (zero) and count **upwards**, one item at a time (i.e. in 'ones') ... 0, 1, 2, 3, 4, 5, 6, etc. When objects are grouped together or when a scale is involved we might count differently, going up in 'tens' for example.

However, there are occasions when we need to count **down** from 0 instead. Numbers below 0 are called **negative** numbers and have a minus sign (-) in front e.g. 0, -1, -2, -3, etc.

A good example of using negative numbers is when we measure temperature. Temperature is measured in degrees Celsius (°C) using a thermometer. Water freezes at 0°C and boils at 100°C. However, the scale on a thermometer includes negative numbers because sometimes we need to measure temperatures below 0°C too. For example, on very cold days in winter the temperature can drop below 0°C e.g. -5°C.

Negative numbers are also used with sums of money quite a lot (see p.22).

❓ Now try these...

Say whether you would expect each of these temperatures to be a positive (+) or a negative (-) value in °C.

1. Normal body temperature
2. Orange juice from a fridge
3. An ice lolly
4. A packet of frozen peas
5. The heating element of an electric fire
6. The foot of a penguin in the snow

Examples

What temperatures are the thermometers showing?

1.

Sunny day 20°C

2.

Ice 0°C

3.

Inside the ice box in a fridge -15°C

Whole Numbers

ℹ️ You need to know...

- **how to order positive and negative numbers**
- **how to add and subtract negative numbers in context.**

Look at the number line below:

smaller -5 -4 -3 -2 -1 0 1 2 3 4 5 bigger

Positive numbers are placed on the number line to the right of 0 (zero). The further to the **right** a number is, the **bigger** it is. Negative numbers are placed on the number line to the left of 0 (zero). The further to the **left** a number is, the **smaller** it is.

Positive and negative whole numbers are called **integers**. If you are given a selection of integers and asked to put them in order of size, you will find a number line very useful.

You can use the number line to add and subtract numbers too. To add, count up the scale (or to the right). To subtract, count down the number scale (or to the left).

Examples

1 Put these numbers in ascending order (smallest first): 5, 8, -4, 0, -1, 7, 3, -3.

First, group all the negative numbers together on the left and the positive numbers on the right then put them in order.

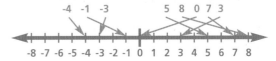

-8 -7 -6 -5 -4 -3 -2 -1 0 1 2 3 4 5 6 7 8

-4, -3, -1, 0, 3, 5, 7, 8

2 On a winter morning, the temperature is -3°C. By lunchtime the temperature has risen to 5°C. What is this change in temperature in °C?

Find the starting temperature (-3°C). Now count up the scale to the finishing temperature (5°C).

Change in temperature = +8°C

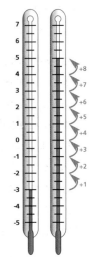

You were counting up the scale, so the answer is positive. If you had been counting down the scale, the answer would have been negative.

❓ Now try these...

1 Put these numbers in descending order (biggest first):
-7, 8, 3, -6, 1, 9, 2

2 Put these numbers in ascending order (smallest first):
5, -9, -2, 0, 3, -7, 6

3 Put these numbers in ascending order (smallest first). You might have to extend the number line or draw a new one to help you.
11, -16, 25, 4, -7, 6, 0, -8, -15, 12

4  Look at this thermometer. It reads 9°C.
- **a)** If the temperature rises by 2°C what will the thermometer read?
- **b)** If it then falls by 15°C what will it read?
- **c)** By how many °C will it have to rise to get back to 9°C?

You need to know...

- **how to add and subtract numbers with two digits mentally**
- **how to add and subtract numbers with three digits using written methods.**

When adding or subtracting whole numbers you need to write the numbers down one beneath the other. It is important to line up the digits according to their place value.

When you begin your calculations, always start on the right-hand side with the units.

Examples

1

```
  H T U
  2 4 7
+   6 2
  ¹
  3 0 9
```

7 + 2 = 9. Write down **9** in the Units column

4 + 6 = 10. Write down **0** in the Tens column and carry **1** into the Hundreds column

2 + 1 = 3. Write down **3** in the Hundreds column

2

```
  H T U
  5 9 8
+ 3 2 5
  ¹ ¹
  9 2 3
```

8 + 5 = 13. Write down **3** in the Units column and carry **1** into the Tens column

9 + 2 + 1 = 12. Write down **2** in the Tens column and carry **1** into the Hundreds column

5 + 3 + 1 = 9. Write down **9** in the Hundreds column

3

```
  H T U
  ³4̶ 2 7
−   3 5
  3 9 2
```

7 − 5 = 2. Write down **2** in the Units column

2 − 3 doesn't work so borrow **1** from the Hundreds column to give **12 − 3 = 9.** Write down **9** in the Tens column

3 − 0 = 3. Write down **3** in the Hundreds column

4

```
  H T U
  5̶6̶ ⁹0̶ ¹5
− 4 6 7
  1 3 8
```

5 − 7 doesn't work. We can't borrow from the Tens column as it's **0** so borrow **1** from the Hundreds to give to the Tens. Now, borrow **1** from the Tens to give **15 − 7 = 8.** Write **8** in the Units

9 − 6 = 3. Write down **3** in the Tens column

5 − 4 = 1. Write down **1** in the Hundreds column

Now try these...

1
```
  1 0 9
+ 5 6 5
```

2
```
  8 7 0
−   9 9
```

3
```
  1 1 7
+ 8 0 6
```

4
```
  5 0 0
− 1 4 2
```

5
```
  6 3 9
+ 1 0 1
```

6
```
  7 3 6
−   3 7
```

7
```
    6 3
+ 7 8 6
```

8
```
  3 0 3
−   2 7
```

9
```
  2 1 8
+ 3 6 9
```

10
```
  9 0 7
− 9 0 5
```

11
```
  3 7 6
+ 7 1 3
```

12
```
  1 0 0
−   6 4
```

Basic Number Skills

- **the multiplication tables up to 10 x 10**
- **that multiplication and division are inverse operations.**

It is important that you know the multiplication tables or 'times tables' up to 10 x 10. You should be able to recall them quickly and accurately in your head. This skill will help you in all other areas of maths.

Division and multiplication are **inverse operations**. That means that they are **opposites**.

When two numbers are multiplied together, the result is called the **product**. Because division is the opposite of multiplication, if you divide the product by one of the original numbers, you will always get the other original number as your answer. Look at the example opposite:

Example

$7 \times 9 = 63$ ➡ therefore ➤ $63 \div 9 = 7$
➤ $63 \div 7 = 9$

x	1	2	3	4	5	6	7	8	9	10
1	1	2	3	4	5	6	7	8	9	10
2	2	4	6	8	10	12	14	16	18	20
3	3	6	9	12	15	18	21	24	27	30
4	4	8	12	16	20	24	28	32	36	40
5	5	10	15	20	25	30	35	40	45	50
6	6	12	18	24	30	36	42	48	54	60
7	7	14	21	28	35	42	49	56	63	70
8	8	16	24	32	40	48	56	64	72	80
9	9	18	27	36	45	54	63	72	81	90
10	10	20	30	40	50	60	70	80	90	100

Now try these...

Complete the following multiplications and divisions without using a calculator (use the multiplication table above if it helps):

1. $\begin{array}{r} 8 \\ \times\ 6 \\ \hline \end{array}$

2. $\begin{array}{r} 7 \\ \times\ 4 \\ \hline \end{array}$

3. $\begin{array}{r} 6 \\ \times\ 10 \\ \hline \end{array}$

4. $\begin{array}{r} 3 \\ \times\ 8 \\ \hline \end{array}$

5. $\begin{array}{r} 9 \\ \times\ 9 \\ \hline \end{array}$

6. $\begin{array}{r} 7 \\ \times\ 8 \\ \hline \end{array}$

7. $6 \overline{)54}$

8. $7 \overline{)42}$

9. $4 \overline{)36}$

10. $3 \overline{)27}$

11. $5 \overline{)25}$

You need to know...

- **how to use written methods of short multiplication and division**
- **how to solve whole number problems involving multiplication and division, including those giving rise to remainders.**

As with addition and subtraction, to multiply two numbers, write them down one beneath the other and line the digits up according to their place values.

When multiplying, always start on the right-hand side with the units.

To divide, use the layout shown below:

$$72 \div 3 \longrightarrow 3\overline{)72}$$

your answer goes here

the number being divided

the number you are dividing by

When you divide, you start with the biggest numbers – on the left-hand side.

You will find multiplication and division much easier if you know your 'times tables' (see p.9).

Now try these...

1
```
    4 9
x     3
———————
```

2
```
    1 3
x     5
———————
```

3
```
    2 0
x     7
———————
```

4
```
    7 8
x     9
———————
```

5   4) 5 2

6   8) 6 5

7   5) 7 3

Examples

1
```
      3 7
x   ₂ 4
———————
    1 4 8
```

4 x 7 = 28. Write down **8** in the Units column and carry the **2** to the Tens column

4 x 3 = 12. Add the 2 to give 12 + 2 = 14. Write down **4** in the Tens column and **1** in the Hundreds column

2
```
      5 7
x   ₆ 9
———————
    5 1 3
```

9 x 7 = 63. Write down **3** in the Units column and carry the **6** to the Tens column

9 x 5 = 45. Add the **6** to give 45 + 6 = 51. Write down **1** in the Tens column and **5** in the Hundreds column

3
```
      1 8
4 ) 7 ³2
```

7 ÷ 4 (or 4 into 7) = 1 remainder 3 (7 – 4 = 3). Write **1** in the Tens column and carry the **3** to the Units column

32 ÷ 4 = 8. Write down **8**

4
```
      0 8
6 ) 4 ⁴8
```

4 ÷ 6 doesn't work so, carry the **4** to the Units column (you can write down **0** if it helps). 48 ÷ 6 = 8. Write **8**

5
```
      1 2 r3
5 ) 6 ¹3
```

6 ÷ 5 = 1 remainder 1 (6 – 5 = 1). Write **1** in the Tens column and carry **1** to the Units column

13 ÷ 5 = 2 remainder 3 (13 – 10 = 3). Write **2** in the Units column and **r3** alongside

6
```
      2 0
3 ) 6 0
```

6 ÷ 3 = 2. Write down **2**

0 ÷ 3 = 0. Write down **0** (You must put this **0** in your answer!)

Basic Number Skills

i You need to know...

- **how to use an appropriate non-calculator method for multiplying and dividing large numbers**
- **how to multiply and divide negative numbers.**

To multiply large numbers, you need to use a method called **long multiplication**.

As shown in Example 1, perform separate multiplications for each digit in the multiplier and then add your results together. Be careful to write down your working at each step of the way, so you don't lose track!

Long division works in the same way as short division (shown on p.10). However, because you are working with large numbers, keep track of your carrying underneath to avoid confusion.

To multiply and divide positive and negative numbers, ignore the signs and calculate as normal. The following rules determine whether the answer is positive or negative:

If the signs are the **same**, the answer is **positive**

$$+ \times + = +$$
$$- \times - = +$$

$$+ \div + = +$$
$$- \div - = +$$

If the signs are **different**, the answer is **negative**

$$+ \times - = -$$
$$- \times + = -$$

$$+ \div - = -$$
$$- \div + = -$$

Examples

1

$$
\begin{array}{r}
361 \\
\times \quad 54 \\
\hline
18^{3}050 \\
+ \ 14^{2}44 \\
\hline
19494
\end{array}
$$

> **54** is **50 + 4** so we start by multiplying **361** by **50** and then by **4** separately

> Start with **361 x 50** – Put a **0** in the Units column and then do **361 x 5. 5 x 1 = 5** write down **5. 5 x 6 = 30** write down **0** and carry the **3** along. **5 x 3 = 15** then add the **3** to give **18**. Write down **18**.

> Now start again to find **361 x 4. 4 x 1 = 4** write down **4. 4 x 6 = 24** write down **4** and carry the **2** along. **4 x 3 = 12** then add the **2** to give **14**. Write down **14**.

> Now add the two answers together (ignore any previous 'carry' numbers!)

2

$$
\begin{array}{r}
038 \\
14\overline{)532} \\
42 \downarrow \\
\hline
112 \\
112 \\
\hline
0
\end{array}
$$

> **14** does not divide into **5** so move on.

> **14** into **53** goes **3** times. **14 x 3 = 42**. Write **42** below the **53** and subtract to give **11**.

> Bring down the **2**. **14** into **112** goes **8** times. **14 x 8 = 112**. Write this below and subtract to give **0**. This means there is no remainder.

> Use the same layouts as examples 1 and 2 then look at the rules on the left to work out the signs

3 $361 \times -54 = -19\,494$

4 $-532 \div -14 = 38$

? Now try these...

1
$$
\begin{array}{r}
549 \\
\times \quad 15 \\
\hline
\end{array}
$$

2
$$
\begin{array}{r}
704 \\
\times \quad -28 \\
\hline
\end{array}
$$

3
$$
\begin{array}{r}
-643 \\
\times \quad 56 \\
\hline
\end{array}
$$

4
$$
\begin{array}{r}
-356 \\
\times \quad -29 \\
\hline
\end{array}
$$

5 $18\overline{)432}$

6 $23\overline{)391}$

7 $17\overline{)952}$

8 $-56\overline{)224}$

9 $25\overline{)625}$

10 $-42\overline{)-882}$

ℹ You need to know...

- **what powers are and how to use them**
- **how to recognise square numbers and cube numbers.**

You use a **power** to show that a number is to be multiplied by itself and by how many times. It is much quicker than writing the multiplications in full. For example, instead of writing...

3 x 3 x 3 x 3 you can simply write **3^4**

> This is called the **power** or **index**. It means 'multiply 3 by itself 4 times'.

Look at the examples below:

6 x 6 = 6^2
> We call power 2 'squaring' so this is '6 squared'

6 x 6 x 6 = 6^3
> We call power 3 'cubing' so this is 'six cubed'

6 x 6 x 6 x 6 = 6^4
> This is read as '6 to the power of 4'

6 x 6 x 6 x 6 x 6 = 6^5
> This is read as '6 to the power of 5'

Numbers made by squaring a number are called **square numbers**. Numbers made by cubing a number are called **cube numbers**. Most calculators have and for squaring and cubing numbers.

Examples

1 The first five square numbers are...

1
$(1^2 = 1\times1)$

4
$(2^2 = 2\times2)$

9
$(3^2 = 3\times3)$

16
$(4^2 = 4\times4)$

25
$(5^2 = 5\times5)$

2 The first five cube numbers are...

1
$(1^3 = 1\times1\times1)$

8
$(2^3 = 2\times2\times2)$

27
$(3^3 = 3\times3\times3)$

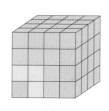 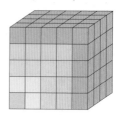

64
$(4^3 = 4\times4\times4)$

125
$(5^3 = 5\times5\times5)$

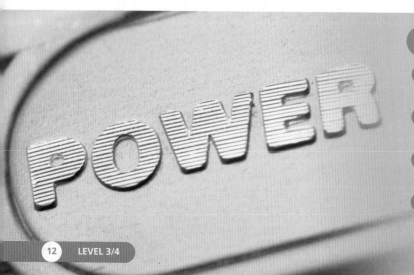

? Now try these...

1 Work out the value of...
a) 4^2 b) 3^3 c) 2^4 d) 1^7

2 Look at Example 1. What are the next 5 square numbers?

3 Look at Example 2. What is the next cube number?

4 Look at the multiplication table on p.9. What do you notice about the numbers on the diagonal (from top left)?

Powers and Roots

You need to know...

- **what a square root is**
- **what a cube root is.**

As with any multiplication, when you square or cube a number the result is called the product.

The reverse of squaring a number is to **square root**. This will take you from the product back to the original number.

You should learn the square roots of the first few square numbers:

$2^2 = 4$	$3^2 = 9$	$4^2 = 16$
$\sqrt{4} = 2$	$\sqrt{9} = 3$	$\sqrt{16} = 4$

$5^2 = 25$	$6^2 = 36$	$7^2 = 49$
$\sqrt{25} = 5$	$\sqrt{36} = 6$	$\sqrt{49} = 7$

$8^2 = 64$	$9^2 = 81$	$10^2 = 100$
$\sqrt{64} = 8$	$\sqrt{81} = 9$	$\sqrt{100} = 10$

The reverse of cubing a number is to **cube root**.

Most calculators should have  and for finding the square root and cube root of a number. Make sure you know how to use yours. Cube root is sometimes written as $x^{\frac{1}{3}}$.

Examples
This is the square root symbol

1. $7^2 = 49$ so $\sqrt{49} = 7$
2. $15^2 = 225$ so $\sqrt{225} = 15$
3. $4^3 = 64$ so $\sqrt[3]{64} = 4$
4. $7^3 = 343$ so $\sqrt[3]{343} = 7$

This is the cube root symbol

? Now try these...

Use a calculator to find...

1. $\sqrt{289}$ 2. $\sqrt{225}$ 3. $\sqrt{400}$
4. $\sqrt{169}$ 5. $\sqrt{324}$ 6. $\sqrt{6.25}$
7. $\sqrt[3]{343}$ 8. $\sqrt[3]{729}$ 9. $\sqrt[3]{2744}$

Without using a calculator find the following square roots (use the multiplication table on p.9 if you get stuck):

10. $\sqrt{36}$ 11. $\sqrt{100}$ 12. $\sqrt{81}$

i You need to know...

- **the difference between odd numbers and even numbers**
- **how to find the factors and multiples of a given number.**

Even numbers are numbers which divide by 2 exactly. They are easy to spot because the digit in the units column is always a … **0, 2, 4, 6 or 8**.

Odd numbers cannot be divided exactly by 2. Odd numbers always end in a … **1, 3, 5, 7 or 9**.

Factors are the numbers which divide exactly into a given number.

Multiples are the numbers produced by multiplying the given number by 1, 2, 3, 4, 5 etc. (i.e. they are your **multiplication tables** – see p.9).

? Now try these...

1 Sort the following numbers into two groups, under the headings Odd and Even.

17, 36, 40, 159, 7, 4444, 305, 200, 11, 28

2 Find all of the factors of…
a) 12   **b)** 33   **c)** 54   **d)** 72   **e)** 100

3 List the first six multiples of…
a) 4   **b)** 8   **c)** 10   **d)** 3   **e)** 7

Examples

1 Circle all the even numbers below. Remember, you only need to look at the last digit in each number!

51   (24) (32)   77   (776)   89   6003

(5010)   8321   (8)   (20 002)   51 431

2 Circle all the odd numbers below.

(11)   80   (5)   (51)   62   (279)   656

(63) (1007)   2888   30 004

3 Find all the factors of…

a) 20

1, 2, 4, 5, 10 and 20
are the factors of 20

b) 15

1, 3, 5 and 15
are the factors of 15

> Most numbers have an even number of factors because they usually occur in pairs e.g. **1 x 15 = 15, 3 x 5 = 15**. This is where it helps to know your multiplication tables.

c) 36

1, 2, 3, 4, 6, 9, 12, 18 and 36
are the factors of 36

> In the last example, 6 is on its own because it is a repeated factor i.e. **6 x 6 = 36**. In other words 36 is a square number (see p.12). All square numbers have an odd number of factors.

4 **a)** Find all the factors of 25
b) Find all the factors of 30
c) Which factor(s) do 25 and 30 have in common?

Types of Number

You need to know...

- **how to identify prime numbers.**

A **prime number** is a number that has exactly two factors – itself and 1. It is worth trying to memorise all the prime numbers under 100 (see below).

1 is not classed as a prime number. It is unique in that it only has one factor and that is 1. **2** is the only even prime number.

Example

Put a circle around all the prime numbers in this number grid.

1	**2**	**3**	4	**5**	6	**7**	8	9	10
11	12	**13**	14	15	16	**17**	18	**19**	20
21	22	**23**	24	25	26	27	28	**29**	30
31	32	33	34	35	36	**37**	38	39	40
41	42	**43**	44	45	46	**47**	48	49	50
51	52	**53**	54	55	56	57	58	**59**	60
61	62	63	64	65	66	**67**	68	69	70
71	72	**73**	74	75	76	77	78	**79**	80
81	82	**83**	84	85	86	87	88	**89**	90
91	92	93	94	95	96	**97**	98	99	100

(Circled numbers shown in bold.)

If you know your multiplication tables you will be able to eliminate all the numbers that are NOT prime numbers easily.

If you suspect a number might be prime, try dividing it by 2, 3, 5, 7, 9 etc. If you can divide it exactly – it's not a prime number!

Now try these...

1. Which of these numbers are prime numbers? (try to answer this question without looking at the chart on this page!)

   11, 33, 23, 73, 91, 39, 101

2. State whether the following are prime numbers and explain your answer.

   a) 94
   b) 29

ⓘ You need to know...

- **how to write fractions correctly**
- **what equivalent fractions are.**

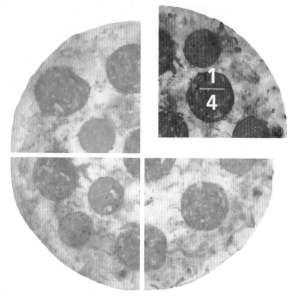

A **fraction** is a part of a whole object. The picture above shows a pizza that has been cut into 4 equal slices (or parts). Each slice can be described as a fraction of the whole pizza, e.g. a quarter of the whole pizza. A quarter is written as $\frac{1}{4}$.

The pizza could have been cut into any number of slices, and this would give us different fractions...

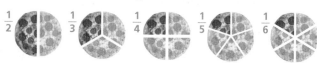

The top number of a fraction is called the **numerator** and it describes how many parts of the object we have. The bottom number of a fraction is called the **denominator** and it describes how many parts make up the whole object.

Sometimes the same amount can be represented by two or more different fractions. These are called equivalent fractions.

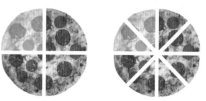

The first pizza shows $\frac{3}{4}$ and the second pizza shows $\frac{6}{8}$. However, the amount of pizza is the same in both pictures so we can say that $\frac{3}{4} = \frac{6}{8}$. They are **equal** or **equivalent fractions**.

Examples

1. Write down what fraction the shaded part of each diagram represents.

   a)    b)   c)

   $\frac{2}{4}$ or $\frac{1}{2}$ $\frac{3}{4}$ $\frac{5}{6}$

2. Shade the diagrams so they represent the fractions given.

   a) $\frac{1}{4}$ b) $\frac{3}{8}$ c) $\frac{2}{6}$ or $\frac{1}{3}$

         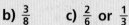

❓ Now try these...

1. Write down what fraction the shaded part of each diagram represents.

   a)   b)   c)

   d)   e)   f)

2. Write down what fraction the shaded part of each diagram represents. Which pair shows equivalent fractions?

   a)   b)   c)

Fractions

i You need to know...

- **how to find equivalent fractions**
- **how to simplify fractions.**

Chains of equivalent fractions can be created by multiplying the numerator and denominator by the same number.

We know that multiplying is the mathematical opposite of dividing, so we can also create a chain of equivalent fractions by dividing the numerator and denominator by the same number. This is known as **simplifying** or **cancelling down**.

When a number consists of a whole number AND a fraction it can be written in two ways: as an **improper fraction** or as a **mixed number**.

Examples

1 Create a chain of equivalent fractions by multiplying the numerator and the denominator of $\frac{1}{2}$ by 3.

$$\overbrace{\frac{1}{2}}^{\times 3} = \overbrace{\frac{3}{6}}^{\times 3} = \overbrace{\frac{9}{18}}^{\times 3} = \frac{27}{54}$$

(× 3 across top, × 3 across bottom)

2 Create a chain of fractions by dividing the numerator and the denominator of $\frac{48}{64}$ by 4.

$$\frac{48}{64} \overset{\div 4}{=} \frac{12}{16} \overset{\div 4}{=} \frac{3}{4}$$

(÷ 4 across top, ÷ 4 across bottom)

3 Simplify (or cancel down) $\frac{100}{140}$.

$$\frac{100}{140} \overset{\div 2}{=} \frac{50}{70} \overset{\div 2}{=} \frac{25}{35} \overset{\div 5}{=} \frac{5}{7}$$

(÷ 2, ÷ 2, ÷ 5 across top and bottom)

4 Look at the pizza.

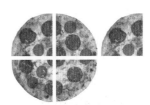

a) How many quarters of pizza are there altogether?

There are 5 quarters of pizza.

b) Write this as a fraction.

$\frac{5}{4}$ **– This is an improper fraction. The numerator is larger than the denominator.**

c) Write this as a mixed number.

$1\frac{1}{4}$ **– This tells us that there is one whole pizza and an extra quarter of pizza.**

? Now try these...

1 By multiplying by 3 each time, find four fractions equivalent to $\frac{2}{5}$.

2 Using any multiplier, find four fractions equivalent to $\frac{1}{7}$.

3 Divide by 2 each time to simplify $\frac{48}{64}$.

4 Describe the quantity represented by the blue areas of these diagrams as both a mixed number and an improper fraction.

a)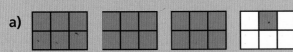

b)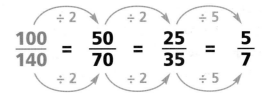

5 Convert $3\frac{1}{4}$ to an improper fraction.

6 Convert  to a mixed number.

7 Convert $5\frac{1}{3}$ to an improper fraction.

8 Convert $\frac{32}{5}$ to a mixed number.

9 Convert $\frac{32}{12}$ to a mixed number and simplify the fraction.

ℹ You need to know...

- **how to add and subtract fractions by writing them with a common denominator**
- **how to multiply and divide fractions.**

To add or subtract fractions, they *must* have the same denominator. If the fractions you are given don't have the same denominator, you will need to find equivalent fractions (see p.17) that do.

The numerators can then simply be added or subtracted. Sometimes the answer can be 'tidied up' by simplifying the fraction or changing an improper fraction to a mixed number.

Fractions can also be multiplied. All you do is multiply the numerators together, and then multiply the denominators together. Remember to simplify your answer.

To divide fractions there is a trick: turn the second fraction upside down and then multiply it with the first, as explained above.

You can use the $\boxed{a\frac{b}{c}}$ button on a calculator to work with fractions. To work out $\frac{3}{4} - \frac{2}{5}$, press **3** $\boxed{a\frac{b}{c}}$ **4** – **2** $\boxed{a\frac{b}{c}}$ **5** = It's as easy as that!
To key in $1\frac{3}{5}$, press **1** $\boxed{a\frac{b}{c}}$ **3** $\boxed{a\frac{b}{c}}$ **5**.
If your calculator has $\boxed{\frac{d}{c}}$ function you can use this to convert a mixed number into an improper fraction. Pressing $\boxed{a\frac{b}{c}}$ again will convert the fraction into a decimal.

Examples

① $\frac{1}{5} + \frac{2}{5} = \frac{3}{5}$

> Both the denominators are **5**, so the addition can be done straight away.

② $\frac{3}{4} - \frac{2}{5}$

$\frac{15}{20} - \frac{8}{20} = \frac{7}{20}$

> **4** and **5** are both factors of **20** so use twentieths.

> Don't forget to multiply the numerator!

③ $\frac{3}{4} + \frac{5}{8}$

$\frac{6}{8} + \frac{5}{8} = \frac{11}{8} = 1\frac{3}{8}$

> **4** and **8** are both factors of **8** so use eighths.

> This is an improper fraction. $\frac{11}{8}$ = **1** remainder **3**

④ $\frac{2}{5} \times \frac{3}{4} = \frac{6}{20} = \frac{3}{10}$

⑤ $\frac{2}{5} \div \frac{2}{3}$

$\frac{2}{5} \times \frac{3}{2} = \frac{6}{10} = \frac{3}{5}$

> $\frac{2}{3}$ becomes $\frac{3}{2}$

> ... now multiply.

⑥ $\frac{2}{3} \div \frac{1}{4}$

$\frac{2}{3} \times \frac{4}{1} = \frac{8}{3} = 2\frac{2}{3}$

> $\frac{1}{4}$ becomes $\frac{4}{1}$

> $\frac{8}{3}$ = **2** remainder **2**

❓ Now try these...

① $\frac{1}{3} + \frac{1}{4} =$

② $\frac{5}{6} - \frac{2}{3} =$

③ $\frac{7}{8} - \frac{1}{2} =$

④ $\frac{5}{9} + \frac{3}{4} =$

⑤ $\frac{2}{3} \times \frac{3}{5} =$

⑥ $\frac{8}{9} \times \frac{1}{4} =$

⑦ $\frac{1}{10} \div \frac{2}{5} =$

⑧ $\frac{3}{5} \div \frac{1}{4} =$

Fractions

You need to know...

- **how to calculate fractional parts of quantities or measurements.**

We often come across fractions in everyday life, for example $\frac{1}{2}$ price sale, $\frac{1}{3}$ extra free, etc. So you need to be able to work out exactly what those fractions represent.

Always read the information you are given carefully. Then decide exactly what you are trying to find e.g. half of £32.00. In maths, 'of' means 'multiply' (**x**) so, to find 'half of £32.00' you need to calculate:

$\frac{1}{2}$ **x £32.00**

To multiply a whole number by a fraction you need to change the whole number into an improper fraction. To do this, you give it a denominator of one:

e.g. **32 as an improper fraction is $\frac{32}{1}$.**

Now you have two fractions you can multiply the numerators together and the denominators together to leave a single fraction:

e.g. $\frac{1}{2}$ **x** $\frac{32}{1}$ = $\frac{32}{2}$

To complete the process, carry out the division:

e.g. $\frac{32}{2}$ = **16 (half of £32.00 is £16.00)**.

Examples

1 Calculate the sale price of this television.

$\frac{1}{2}$ **of £250** = $\frac{1}{2}$ **x 250**

$= \frac{1}{2}$ **x** $\frac{250}{1}$

$= \frac{250}{2}$

$= $ **£125**

2 Calculate the total weight of this box of cereal.

$\frac{1}{3}$ **of 480g** = $\frac{1}{3}$ **x 480**

$= \frac{1}{3}$ **x** $\frac{480}{1}$

$= \frac{480}{3}$

$= $ **160g**

So you get **480g + 160g = 640g**

3 Work out $\frac{3}{5}$ of £120.

$\frac{3}{5}$ **x £120** = $\frac{3}{5}$ **x** $\frac{120}{1}$

$= \frac{360}{5}$

$= $ **£72**

Now try these...

1 The price of a car is reduced by $\frac{1}{4}$ in a sale. If the car's original price was £12 800...
   a) how much is the discount?
   b) what is the sale price?

2 A school library increases its stock of books by $\frac{1}{6}$. If it had 960 books originally...
   a) how many new books has it bought?
   b) what is the new total number of books in stock?

3 A new light bulb is found to last only $\frac{3}{4}$ as long as it should. If it should have lasted 420 hours, how long does it actually last?

4 A shirt is reduced by $\frac{1}{3}$ in a sale. If it originally cost £39.00...
   a) how much is the discount?
   b) what is the sale price?

ℹ You need to know...

- **how the place value table can be extended for decimals**
- **about recurring and terminating decimals.**

We can extend our place value table to the right for amounts less than 1 whole. A decimal point (.) is used to show where the whole part of the number ends and the decimal part begins.

It is vital that the decimal point is positioned correctly as moving it one place to the left or right alters the size of the number by ten times! Zeros are just as important e.g. £1.08 million is much less than £1.8 million (there's a difference of £720 000!).

To order decimals by size, put all the numbers in a list, making sure the decimal points line up. Look at each column of digits in turn (working from left to right), searching for the biggest numbers.

Place Value of Digits						Number
10 Tens	**1** Units	**.** DECIMAL POINT	$\frac{1}{10}$ Tenths	$\frac{1}{100}$ Hundredths	$\frac{1}{1000}$ Thousandths	
	0		6			Zero point six
	1		5			One point five
2	3		0	7		Twenty three point zero seven
	9		1	1	1	Nine point one one one
3	8		8	0	4	Thirty eight point eight zero four

Some decimals have digits or sequences of digits which repeat themselves without end. These are called recurring decimals. Some recurring decimals are...

- **0.33333333...** this is written as **0.3̇** because the 3 is repeated

- **0.27272727...** this is written as **0.2̇7̇** because the 27 is repeated

- **0.571482571482571482...** is written as **0.5̇71482̇** because the 571482 is repeated

Decimals which have an exact value are called terminating decimals. Some terminating decimals are... 0.5, 0.65, 0.0008.

Example

Put these decimals in descending order (biggest first)... **0.72, 0.27, 2.7, 0.027, 0.702**

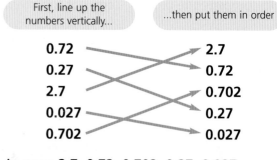

First, line up the numbers vertically... ...then put them in order

0.72	2.7
0.27	0.72
2.7	0.702
0.027	0.27
0.702	0.027

Answer: **2.7, 0.72, 0.702, 0.27, 0.027**

❓ Now try these...

1. Put these amounts of money in ascending order.
£3.17, £3.71, £7.31, £0.37, £7.13, £1.73

2. Put these decimals in descending order.
0.123, 0.213, 0.132, 0.312, 0.231, 0.321

3. Use a dot (˙) to write these recurring decimals correctly:
a) 0.666666....
b) 0.85714285714285....
c) 0.818181818181....

Decimals

ℹ You need to know...

- **how to add and subtract decimals of up to two decimal places.**

When adding or subtracting decimals you use the same method as for whole numbers (see p.8).

Before you begin, make sure the decimal points are lined up and put in zeros to fill any gaps.

Always start with the column on the right-hand side (in the examples shown below, that's the Hundredths ($\frac{1}{100}$) column) and don't forget to bring down the decimal point!

Examples

1

| H | T | U | $\frac{1}{10}$ | $\frac{1}{100}$ |

$$3\,4\,2\,.\,7\,9$$
$$+\ \ \ 1\,7\,.\,6\,0$$
$$\overline{3\,6\,0\,.\,3\,9}$$

Add the **0** if it helps. **9 + 0 = 9**. Write **9** in the Hundredths column

7 + 6 = 13. Write **3** in the Tenths column and carry **1** into the Units column. Don't forget to bring down the decimal point!

2 + 7 + 1 = 10. Write **0** in the Units column and carry **1** into the Tens column

4 + 1 + 1 = 6. Write **6** in the Tens column

3 + 0 = 3. Write **3** in the Hundreds column

2

| T | U | $\frac{1}{10}$ | $\frac{1}{100}$ |

$$\overset{4}{5}\overset{13}{4}\,.\,\overset{1}{1}\,7$$
$$-\,1\,8\,.\,2\,5$$
$$\overline{3\,5\,.\,9\,2}$$

7 – 5 = 2. Write **2** in the Hundredths column

Borrow **1** from the Units column to give **11 – 2 = 9.** Write **9** in the Tenths column

Borrow **1** from the Tens column to give **13 – 8 = 5.** Write **5** in the Units column

4 – 1 = 3. Write **3** in the Tens column

❓ Now try these...

1
$$\begin{array}{r} 8\,3\,1 \\ 1\,0\,1 \\ +\ \ \ \ 6\,9 \\ \hline \end{array}$$

2
$$\begin{array}{r} 1\,0\,0\,5 \\ +\ \ \ 5\,6\,5 \\ \hline \end{array}$$

3
$$\begin{array}{r} 5\,0\,0\,6 \\ -\,1\,4\,2\,9 \\ \hline \end{array}$$

4
$$\begin{array}{r} 1\,8\,9\,.\,5 \\ +\ \ \ 1\,8\,.\,7\,2 \\ \hline \end{array}$$

5
$$\begin{array}{r} 1\,0\,9\,2\,.\,5 \\ -\ \ \ 1\,9\,9\,.\,4 \\ \hline \end{array}$$

6
$$\begin{array}{r} 5\,0\,7\,5\,.\,1\,6 \\ -\ \ \ 3\,0\,1\,.\,0\,8 \\ \hline \end{array}$$

7
$$\begin{array}{r} 1\,1\,1\,.\,1\,1 \\ +\ \ 9\,9\,.\,9\,9 \\ \hline \end{array}$$

8
$$\begin{array}{r} 1\,1\,1\,.\,1\,1 \\ -\ \ 9\,9\,.\,9\,9 \\ \hline \end{array}$$

9
$$\begin{array}{r} 3\,2\,9\,.\,6\,3 \\ -\ \ 5\,6\,.\,6\,2 \\ \hline \end{array}$$

10
$$\begin{array}{r} 2\,0\,9\,.\,9\,9 \\ -\ \ \ 3\,2\,.\,6\,9 \\ \hline \end{array}$$

11
$$\begin{array}{r} 4\,0\,6\,7\,.\,3 \\ +\ \ \ 1\,4\,1\,.\,7 \\ \hline \end{array}$$

12
$$\begin{array}{r} 1\,3\,5\,4\,.\,6 \\ -\ \ \ 1\,2\,3\,.\,0\,2 \\ \hline \end{array}$$

ℹ You need to know...

- **how to understand and use decimals and negative numbers.**

A common use of decimals is in dealing with money and bank accounts. Sums of money are written to 2 decimal places (2 d.p). The whole numbers represent pounds and the decimals represent pence.

Money that is put into an account is called a **credit**. Money taken out is called a **debit** (or a withdrawal). Withdrawals normally appear as negative numbers. The amount of money remaining in the account is called the **balance**. If a sum of money larger than the balance is taken out, the new balance will be negative.

Examples

Look at this bank statement.

1. How much money was in the account at the beginning of June?
   £221.59

2. How much money was received as a salary in June?
   £550.00

3. After the CHQ00031 transaction, was the account balance positive or negative?
   Negative

4. If no more transactions take place before 6 July what will the account balance be after July's salary of £550.00 is received?
   -£139.78 + £550.00 = £410.22

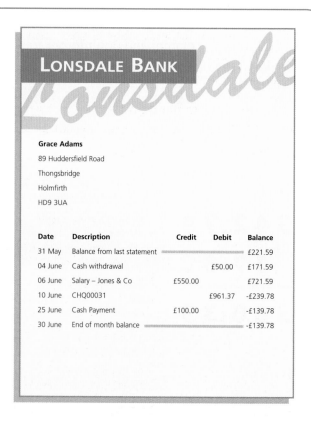

LONSDALE BANK

Grace Adams
89 Huddersfield Road
Thongsbridge
Holmfirth
HD9 3UA

Date	Description	Credit	Debit	Balance
31 May	Balance from last statement			£221.59
04 June	Cash withdrawal		£50.00	£171.59
06 June	Salary – Jones & Co	£550.00		£721.59
10 June	CHQ00031		£961.37	-£239.78
25 June	Cash Payment	£100.00		-£139.78
30 June	End of month balance			-£139.78

❓ Now try these...

1. Write the following amounts as pounds and pence using decimals:
   a) three pounds and fifty pence
   b) eleven pounds and two pence
   c) one hundred and fifty pence
   d) two hundred and one pence
   e) nine hundred pounds and seventy pence
   f) twenty three pounds and twenty three pence

2. David receives a bank statement saying he is overdrawn by twenty five pounds and fifty pence.
   a) write this number as it would appear on the statement.
   b) how much money does David need to pay into the account to take the balance to...
   i) £0.00?   ii) £10.00?   iii) £50.00?

i You need to know...

- **how to multiply and divide decimals by 10, 100 and 1000.**

To **multiply** a decimal by 10, the digits remain the same but you move the decimal point one place to the **right**. To multiply by 100, you move the decimal point two places to the right. To multiply by 1000, you move it three places etc...

The trick is to count the number of zeros and then move the decimal point to the right by the same number of places.

In the same way, to **divide** a decimal by 10, 100 or 1000 you move the decimal point to the **left** by one, two or three places.

Examples

1 Multiply 21.375 by 10, 100 and 1000.

$$21.375 \times 10 = 213.75$$
$$21.375 \times 100 = 2137.5$$
$$21.375 \times 1000 = 21375.0$$

> There's no need for the decimal point in the last example, but you can put it in if it helps.

2 Multiply 425.6 by 10, 100 and 1000.

$$425.6 \div 10 = 42.56$$
$$425.6 \div 100 = 4.256$$
$$425.6 \div 1000 = 0.4256$$

> You need a **zero** here to show there's no whole number.

3 Divide 68.75 by 10, 100 and 1000.

$$068.75 \div 1000 = 0.06875$$

> This **zero** is vital. Without it all the place values would change.

? Now try these...

1. Multiply 25.189 by 10, 100 and 1000
2. Divide 13.27 by 10, 100 and 1000
3. Multiply 0.0135 by 10, 100 and 1000
4. Divide 475.6 by 10, 100 and 1000
5. Multiply 1.111 by 10, 100 and 1000
6. Divide 1.111 by 10, 100 and 1000
7. Multiply 63.98 by 100 and then divide by 1000. What is the answer?

...know...

- **how to multiply and divide decimals of up to two decimal places by whole numbers**
- **how to multiply decimals of up to two decimal places by other decimals.**

The method for multiplying and dividing decimals by a whole number is the same as for multiplying or dividing two whole numbers (see p.9-11). You just need to remember to bring the decimal point up/down to your answer and line it up with the decimal point in the question.

To multiply two decimals together, treat them as whole numbers and perform the multiplication as you would normally. When you have an answer, put the decimal point in position by counting the total number of decimal places in the original numbers.

Examples

1
```
   39.28
x  5 1 4 6
--------
 235.68
```

2
```
      8
x   0.5
------
    4.0
```

3
```
   2.73
x    18
------
  27 30
  21⁵8²4
    1
------
  49.14
```

4
```
      04.06
8 )32.48
   32
   ---
     048
      48
      --
       0
```

5
```
      02.2
6 )13.2
   12
   --
    12
    12
    --
     0
```

6
```
      01.6
12 )19.2
    12
    --
     72
     72
     --
      0
```

7
```
   7.56
x   9.2
```

Remove the decimal points…

```
      756
x      92
------
   68⁵0⁵40
   15¹1¹2
------
   69.552
    3  2  1
```

Now count the total number of decimal places in the question. **7.56** has 2 decimal places and **9.2** has 1 decimal place, making a total of **3**. So, the answer is **69.552**.

24 LEVEL 5/6

Decimals

You need to know...

- **how to divide decimals of up to two decimal places by other decimals.**

The easiest way to divide a decimal by another decimal is to turn the number you are dividing by into a whole number. To do this, multiply both numbers in the calculation by 10 or 100 (depending on how many decimal places the divider has).

As long as you do the same to both numbers, your final answer will not be affected.

Remember: to multiply by 10, you need to move the decimal point one place to the right. To multiply by 100, you move it two places to the right (see p.5).

Once you have done this, divide the numbers as before (see p.11). Just make sure you bring the decimal point up to the answer and line it up with the decimal point in the question (if there is one).

Examples

1 1.92 ÷ 1.2

1.92 x 10 = 19.2

1.2 x 10 = 12

Multiply both numbers by 10

```
      0 1.6
12 ) 1 9.2
     1 2
     ───
       7 2
       7 2
       ───
         0
```

Now divide as normal

2 45.2 ÷ 0.5

45.2 x 10 = 452

0.5 x 10 = 5

Multiply both numbers by 10

```
      0 9 0.4
5 ) 4 5 2.0
    4 5
    ───
      0 2 0
        2 0
        ───
          0
```

Now divide as normal

? Now try these...

1
```
  1 3 . 6
x       5
─────────
```

2
```
  2 2 . 4 8
x         7
───────────
```

3
```
  1 5 8 . 4
x       3 . 6
─────────────
```

4
```
  2 9 . 5 8
x   0 . 4 2
───────────
```

5 8) 68.48

6 14) 2.24

7 1.8) 6.48

8 0.3) 1.335

9 0.25) 5.5

10 0.1) 99.9

11 1.25) 4.25

You need to know...

- **that 'percentage' means 'number of parts per 100'.**

Percentages are simply fractions that are always 'out of 100'. This means that the denominator is always 100.

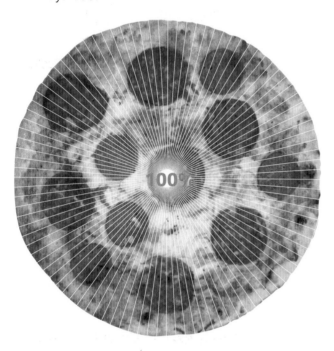

This pizza has been cut into 100 slices. Each slice is $\frac{1}{100}$ or 1% (one percent) and the whole pizza is **100 x 1% = 100%**.

Look at these common percentages...

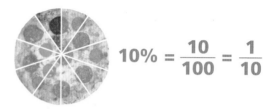 $10\% = \dfrac{10}{100} = \dfrac{1}{10}$

 $20\% = \dfrac{20}{100} = \dfrac{2}{10} = \dfrac{1}{5}$

 $30\% = \dfrac{30}{100} = \dfrac{3}{10}$

 $40\% = \dfrac{40}{100} = \dfrac{4}{10} = \dfrac{2}{5}$

 $50\% = \dfrac{50}{100} = \dfrac{5}{10} = \dfrac{1}{2}$

Example

At lunchtime, Paul eats 40% of a cake. His brother James eats 25% for tea. What percentage of the cake is left?

40% + 25% = 65%

100% − 65% = 35% left

? Now try these...

1. A car is on sale with a 24% discount. What percentage of the original amount do you have to pay?
2. What percentage of this chocolate bar has been unwrapped? (Hint – you could think of the fraction first then use the pizzas above to get the percentage).

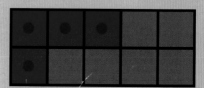

Percentages

You need to know...

- **how to find the exact amount or quantity represented by a percentage.**

Percentages are another kind of number that you frequently come across in everyday life, e.g. 50% extra free, 40% off marked price. To understand them, you need to be able to calculate the exact amounts the percentages represent.

Start by writing the percentage as a fraction. Once you have done that, the method is the same as for finding a fraction of a whole (see p.16).

Remember that 'of' means 'multiply' (x).

? Now try these...

1. Work out 85% of £600.
2. What is 25% of 250g?
3. Calculate 4% of 750ml.
4. Work out 98% of 100m.
5. A holiday is reduced by 30% in a last-minute offer. If the cost was originally £2400 work out the saving and the actual cost of the holiday.
6. The weekly attendance of supporters at a football club is increased by 15%. If 1200 people attended originally, how many more people are now attending and what is the new attendance?

Examples

1

What will this shirt cost after the reduction?

40% of £9 means $\frac{40}{100}$ x £9

$\frac{40}{100}$ x £9 = $\frac{40}{100}$ x $\frac{9}{1}$ = $\frac{360}{100}$ = **£3.60 saved**

The shirt will cost **£9 – £3.60 = £5.40**

2

What is the total weight of this cheese?

50% of 350g means $\frac{50}{100}$ x 350

$\frac{50}{100}$ x 350 = $\frac{50}{100}$ x $\frac{350}{1}$ = $\frac{17\,500}{100}$ = **175g**

So the cheese weighs **350g + 175g = 525g**

3

What is 45% of £1.80?

45% of £1.80 means $\frac{45}{100}$ x 180p (£1.80 = 180p)

$\frac{45}{100}$ x 180 = $\frac{45}{100}$ x $\frac{180}{1}$ = $\frac{8100}{100}$ = **81p**

Examples

(1) Express 200m as a percentage of 4km.

> The units must be the same, so convert **4km** into **m** (see p.60): **4 x 1000m = 4000m**

> $\frac{200}{4000}$ means '**200m out of 4000m**'

$$\frac{200}{4000} \times \frac{100}{1} = \frac{20\,000}{4000} = 5\%$$

(2) A box of cereal weighs 320g. As part of a special offer, its weight is increased to 400g. Express this increase as a percentage of the original weight.

> First calculate the actual increase:

400g – 320g = 80g

> So, you need to find **80g** out of **320g** as a percentage:

$$\frac{80}{320} \times \frac{100}{1} = \frac{8000}{320} = 25\%$$

(3) A man buys a radio for £20. After a year, he sells it on the internet for £12.50. Calculate the loss (decrease) as a percentage of the original cost.

> Calculate the actual loss:

£20.00 – £12.50 = £7.50

> Then the percentage loss:

$$\frac{£7.50}{£20.00} \times \frac{100}{1} = \frac{750}{20} = 37.5\%$$

ℹ You need to know...

- **how to express an amount or quantity as a percentage of another**
- **how to use percentages to compare quantities.**

Any quantity that represents part of a whole e.g. '8 out of 10', can be written as a percentage.

Start by writing the numbers as a fraction. The number that represents the whole always goes on the bottom e.g. $\frac{8}{10}$

Then multiply the fraction by 100%. Remember, when you multiply a fraction by a whole number you change the whole number into an improper fraction first (see p.17) e.g. $\frac{8}{10} \times \frac{100}{1} = \frac{800}{10} = 80\%$

Percentages are a good way of comparing different amounts or quantities, because the 0-100% scale is easy to understand.

Percentages also provide a useful way of describing increases and decreases.

? Now try these...

(1) Express 42 as a percentage of 210.

(2) Express 12cm as a percentage of 120cm.

(3) Express 330ml as a percentage of 1000ml.

(4) A student gets 36 out of a possible 80 marks in Maths and 24 out of a possible 60 marks in Science.
a) Express these results as percentages.
b) Which subject did they do best in?

(5) An antique clock is bought for £5000. It is later sold for £5400. What is the profit (increase) as a percentage of the original cost?

(6) A jockey weighs in at 63kg. He has to get down to 56kg for an important race. What is this decrease in weight as a percentage of his current weight?

(7) A 25g bag of crisps contains 5g of fat. What is this as a percentage?

Percentages

i You need to know...

- **how to find and use equivalent fractions, decimals and fractions.**

It will help you a great deal if you learn the equivalent decimal and percentage values for the most common fractions.

You will come across lots of different fractions, decimals and percentages though so it is important you know how to convert from one to another.

The diagram below shows the rules you need to follow.

Fraction	Decimal	Percentage
1	1.0	100%
$\frac{3}{4}$	0.75	75%
$\frac{1}{2}$	0.5	50%
$\frac{1}{3}$	0.3	33%
$\frac{1}{4}$	0.25	25%
$\frac{1}{5}$	0.2	20%
$\frac{1}{10}$	0.1	10%

Example

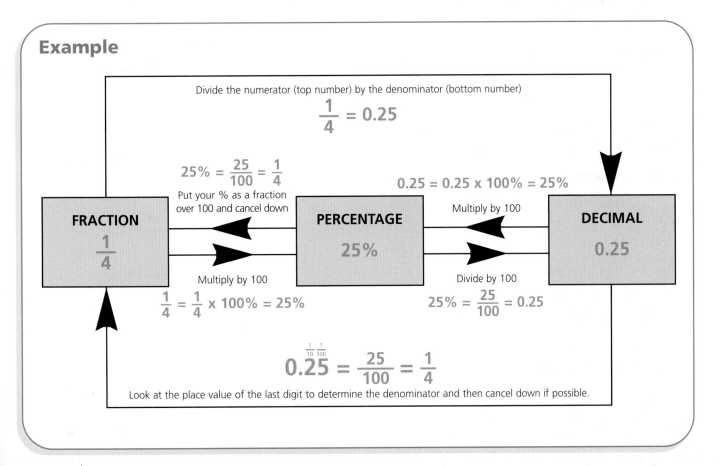

Divide the numerator (top number) by the denominator (bottom number)

$$\frac{1}{4} = 0.25$$

$25\% = \frac{25}{100} = \frac{1}{4}$

Put your % as a fraction over 100 and cancel down

$0.25 = 0.25 \times 100\% = 25\%$

Multiply by 100

FRACTION $\frac{1}{4}$ **PERCENTAGE** 25%   **DECIMAL** 0.25

Multiply by 100

$\frac{1}{4} = \frac{1}{4} \times 100\% = 25\%$

Divide by 100

$25\% = \frac{25}{100} = 0.25$

$$0.\overset{\frac{1}{10}\,\frac{1}{100}}{25} = \frac{25}{100} = \frac{1}{4}$$

Look at the place value of the last digit to determine the denominator and then cancel down if possible.

? Now try these...

1. Convert $\frac{3}{5}$ to a decimal and then to a percentage.
2. What is 65% as a fraction and a decimal?
3. Express 0.32 as a percentage and as a fraction simplified to its lowest terms.
4. Convert $\frac{3}{8}$ to a decimal and then to a percentage.
5. Re-write 36% as a fraction in its lowest terms and as a decimal.
6. Give 1.25 as a percentage and as a mixed number (fraction).

ⓘ You need to know...

- **how to use your maths skills in everyday situations.**

Your knowledge of maths will help you in everyday life, for example, if you need to check a household bill or calculate the total cost of a purchase.

You may also come across questions based on situations like these in the National Curriculum Tests, so it is important that you can tackle them confidently.

Examples

① Fill in the gaps to complete the gas bill below:

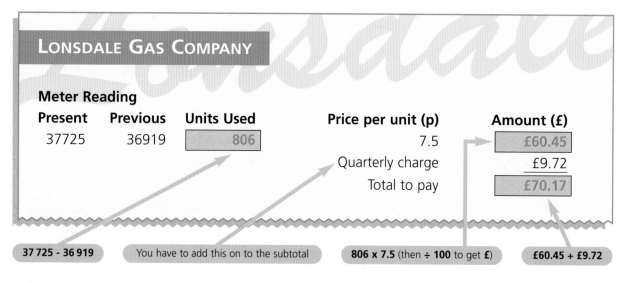

LONSDALE GAS COMPANY

Meter Reading

Present	Previous	Units Used		Price per unit (p)	Amount (£)
37725	36919	806		7.5	£60.45
				Quarterly charge	£9.72
				Total to pay	£70.17

37 725 - 36 919   You have to add this on to the subtotal   806 x 7.5 (then ÷ 100 to get £)   £60.45 + £9.72

② A carpet is bought by paying a cash deposit of £75 and making monthly payments of £9.50 for 10 months. What is the total cost of the carpet?

	£95.00	10 x £9.50
+	£75.00	Paid as a deposit
Total	**£170.00**	

❓ Now try these...

① Look at Example 1. What would the figures in the Amount column become if the Gas Company raised the Price per unit to 8.5p and reduced the Quarterly Charge to £8.60?

② A newly married couple buy a house. They pay a deposit of £35 000 and arrange to pay off the remainder in monthly instalments of £270 for 20 years. What is the total cost of the house?

③ A car rental company hires out cars for £25 per day. All customers have to pay an additional £30 fuel charge. What is the total cost of hiring a car for 5 days?

④ A mobile phone company charges its customers £8.50 per month for line rental and 2p per minute for calls. In one month a customer makes 185 minutes of calls. What is their total bill for that month?

Everyday Calculations

ℹ You need to know...

- **how to solve problems involving VAT and simple interest.**

Value Added Tax (VAT) is payable on most goods we buy. Often it is included in the price. Sometimes, however, it needs to be added on to find the total cost of the product.

In the UK, VAT is currently calculated as 17.5% of the product's value.

Interest is an additional sum of money, paid to you for investing money (e.g. putting it into a bank account) or charged to you for borrowing money over a period of time.

Simple interest means that the amount of interest paid each year is calculated from the original sum of money invested or borrowed.

? Now try these...

1. A DVD player is advertised as costing £90 + VAT. What is the total price to be paid?
2. A phone company charges 5p per minute for calls to the USA, plus VAT. What is the total cost for a call lasting 20 minutes?
3. Louise invests £3500 in an account paying 5% interest per annum (per annum means 'each year'). If she leaves the money there, how much money will she have in the account after 3 years?

Examples

1

A CD player is priced at £50 + VAT. What is the total price to be paid?

17.5% of £50 is $\frac{17.5}{100} \times \frac{50}{1} = \frac{875}{100} = £8.75$

So, the total cost of the CD player is...
£50 + £8.75 = £58.75

2

Mrs Mears wins £1000 and puts it into an account that pays 6% interest per year. If she leaves it there, how much money will she have in the account after 2 years?

6% of £1000 is $\frac{6}{100} \times \frac{1000}{1} = \frac{6000}{100} = £60$ interest per year.

> With simple interest the interest gained (**£60**) is not added to the amount invested so it does not earn interest in the next year.

So, after 2 years she has...
£1000 + £60 + £60 = £1120

| original sum | 1st year's interest | 2nd year's interest |

Everyday Calculations

ℹ You need to know...

- **how to compare quantities and amounts efficiently.**

When you go shopping, the same product is often available in a variety of sizes at different prices. To find out which one offers the best value for money, you need to be able to make accurate comparisons between them.

Likewise, if you require a service like a plumber, window cleaner, taxi etc. you will find that different companies have different rates and fixed costs. Again, you need to be able to determine which company offers the best value for money if you don't want to be short changed!

? Now try these...

1. A supermarket sells lemonade in 2 litre bottles and 3 litre bottles. If 2 litre bottles cost 61p and 3 litre bottles cost 84p which offers the best value?

2. Katie the Plumber charges a £50 call out fee, plus £15 per hour. Perfect Pipes charges a £60 call out fee, plus £12 per hour.
   a) Work out the cost for each plumber to do 1, 2, 3, 4, 5 and 6 hours' work.
   b) Who would be the cheapest for a 3 hour job?
   c) Who would be the cheapest for a 7 hour job?

Examples

1. Uncle Don's Meat Pies are available in two sizes: 300g and 500g. If a 300g pie costs £1.26 and a 500g pie costs £1.95. Which offers the best value for money?

   Work out how much 100g of each pie costs...

   $$\frac{300g}{100g} = 3 \quad \text{so} \quad \frac{£1.26}{3} = 0.42 \quad \text{i.e. 42p per 100g}$$

   $$\frac{500g}{100g} = 5 \quad \text{so} \quad \frac{£1.95}{5} = 0.39 \quad \text{i.e. 39p per 100g}$$

   The 500g pies are the best value.

2. Mark's Taxis charge a fixed amount of £3 per journey, plus £2 per mile. Helen's Cabs only charge a fixed amount of £1, but £2.50 per mile. Work out which taxi company is the cheapest for journeys of 1, 2, 3, 4, 5 and 10 miles.

Journey (miles)	Mark's Taxis	Helen's Cabs
1	(1 x £2) + £3 = £5.00	(1 x £2.50) + £1 = £3.50
2	(2 x £2) + £3 = £7.00	(2 x £2.50) + £1 = £6.00
3	(3 x £2) + £3 = £9.00	(3 x £2.50) + £1 = £8.50
4	(4 x £2) + £3 = £11.00	(4 x £2.50) + £1 = £11.00
5	(5 x £2) + £3 = £13.00	(5 x £2.50) + £1 = £13.50
10	(10 x £2) + £3 = £23.00	(10 x £2.50) + £1 = £26.00

Both taxi companies charge the same amount for a 4 mile journey.

Order of Operations

Examples

① 7 + 3 x 2 — Do the multiplication first so, 3 x 2 = 6 ...

7 + 6 = 13 — ... and then the addition

② 14 − (6 + 3) — Do the brackets first so, 6 + 3 = 9 ...

14 − 9 = 5 — ... and then the subtraction

③ 3^2 x (6 − 4) — Do the brackets first so, 6 − 4 = 2 ...

3^2 x 2 — ... then the square, $3^2 = 9$ ...

9 x 2 = 18 — ... and then the multiplication

④ $\dfrac{5 - 17}{2 \times 3}$ — A divide line like this makes the numerator and denominator act as if they were in brackets, so do them first before dividing

$\dfrac{5 - 17}{6}$ — Do the multiplication first so, 2 x 3 = 6 ...

... then the subtraction, 5 − 17 = − 12 ...

$\dfrac{-12}{6} = -2$ — ... and then the division

ℹ You need to know...

* the correct order in which to carry out mathematical operations when solving problems
* how to use brackets correctly.

When a calculation involves more than one operation, you must carry them out in the correct order – this is not necessarily the order in which they appear.

BIDMAS

Brackets

Indices (or powers)

Divisions and **M**ultiplications (in any order)

Additions and **S**ubtractions (in any order)

Putting brackets into a calculation tells people that they need to perform that part of the calculation before anything else. It can make a big difference to the final answer so make sure you put them in the right place!

? Now try these...

Calculate...

1. 8 − 3 x 2
2. 15 − (2 + 4)
3. 5^2 − 2 x (4 − 1)
4. $\dfrac{5 + 11}{12 - 2^2}$
5. 7 − 4 x 3 + 2
6. 7 x 4 − 3 x 2
7. 13 − 3 x 4 + 3

Put the brackets into this calculation so that the answer is ...

a) 43
b) 70
c) 4

i You need to know...

- **what a ratio is**
- **how to simplify a ratio.**

A ratio is a means of comparing two or more related quantities.

Ratios are usually only written with whole numbers. A colon (:) is used to separate the different quantities.

For example, in one week, the ratio of working weekdays to weekend days is **5 : 2**, since there are 5 weekdays and 2 weekend days. The colon is read as 'to' so, 5 : 2 is read as 'five to two'.

Ratios can be simplified in a similar way to fractions, but you must remember that fractions and ratios are different – they give different information about a situation.

In the example above, the ratio of weekdays to weekend days is 5 : 2. However, the fraction of weekdays is $\frac{5}{7}$ and the fraction of weekend days is $\frac{2}{7}$ as there are 7 days in a week.

Monday	Tuesday	Wednesday	Thursday	Friday	Saturday	Sunday
1	2	3	4	5	6	7
8	9	10	11	12	13	14
15	16	17	18	19	20	21
22	23	24	25	26	27	28

Examples

1 Simplify the ratio 10 : 6.

As long as you divide both parts of the ratio by the same number, the meaning of the ratio will stay the same.

$÷2$ **10 : 6** $÷2$
     = 5 : 3

> **2** is a common factor of **10** and **6**, so divide both numbers by **2**

2 In a pile of bricks, there are 15 red ones and 5 yellow ones.

a) What is the ratio of red to yellow bricks?

     red : yellow
$÷5$ **15 : 5** $÷5$
     = 3 : 1

> **5** is a common factor of **15** and **5**, so divide both numbers by **5**

b) What is the ratio of yellow to red bricks?

     yellow : red
$÷5$ **5 : 15** $÷5$
     = 1 : 3

> Put the items in the ratio in the same order they are written

3 In a maths class, $\frac{2}{5}$ of the pupils are boys. What is the ratio of boys to girls?

     boys : girls
       2 : 3
     (not 2 : 5!)

> If $\frac{2}{5}$ are boys then $\frac{3}{5}$ must be girls.

? Now try these...

1 Simplify the following ratios:

a) 6 : 2   **b)** 9 : 18   **c)** 25 : 10   **d)** 3 : 12

e) 32 : 8 : 16   **f)** 4 : 16 : 8   **g)** 9 : 27 : 45

2 $\frac{4}{7}$ of Anna's toy animals are farm animals, the rest are zoo animals.

a) What is the ratio of farm animals to zoo animals?

b) What is the ratio of zoo animals to farm animals?

Ratio

You need to know...

- **how to solve simple problems involving ratio and direct proportion.**

Because the numbers in a ratio represent parts in a whole, a ratio can tell you how to share something out or divide it up.

In simple terms, if you had 5 sweets and were told to share them between you and a friend in the ratio of 3 : 2, you would get 3 of the 5 sweets and your friend would get 2.

Ratios are also very useful when you need to increase or decrease quantities whilst keeping the proportions the same.

Examples

1

Mavis and Albert enter a prize draw. Mavis buys 5 tickets and Albert buys 3. They agree to share any prize money in the ratio of the number of tickets bought. How much money would each person receive if they won £240?

The ratio of tickets bought is...

Mavis : Albert

  5 : 3

  5 + 3 = 8 tickets

> Add together to find the total number of tickets bought

  £240 ÷ 8 = £30

> prize money per ticket

Therefore...

Mavis receives 5 x £30 = £150

Albert receives 3 x £30 = £90

> Check your answer
> **£150 + £90 = £240**

2

Auntie Edna makes her famous '2, 4, 6, 8' cake using the recipe alongside. The recipe makes enough cake for 12 people. How much of each ingredient would be needed to make enough cake for 18 people?

> **'2 4 6 8' CAKE**
> 2 eggs mixed with 2 cups of milk
> 400g margarine
> 600g sugar
> 800g flour

Start with the ratio **12 : 18**

> You could divide the quantities by **12** to find the amount needed for one person and then multiply it by **18**. However, this would be tricky without a calculator.

To make things easier, simplify the ratio:

÷6   **12 : 18**   ÷6

     = 2 : 3

> **6** is a common factor of **12** and **18**, so divide both numbers by **6**:

> Now, divide each quantity by **2** and then multiply by **3**:

2 eggs	(÷ 2 x 3 =)	**3 eggs**
2 cups of milk	(÷ 2 x 3 =)	**3 cups of milk**
400g margarine	(÷ 2 x 3 =)	**600g margarine**
600g sugar	(÷ 2 x 3 =)	**900g sugar**
800g flour	(÷ 2 x 3 =)	**1200g flour**

? Now try these...

1 Three boys aged 6, 8 and 10 share out their sweets in the ratio of their ages. If they have 36 sweets in total, how many does each boy get?

2 A pudding which serves 8 people requires 200g of dried mixed fruit and 300g of sugar. What quantity of each of these ingredients would be needed to make enough pudding for just 6 people?

You need to know...

- **how to round numbers to the nearest 10, 100 and 1000.**

It is not always necessary to work with exact figures, especially when very large (or very small) numbers are involved.

In these situations you can **round** the number to a suitable level of accuracy e.g. the nearest 10, 100 or 1000. Rounding numbers in this way is sometimes called **approximating**.

For example, the Isle of Man has a population of 75 049. However, you could say it is approximately 75 000 – this number describes the size of the population without being confusing.

To round a number to the nearest 10, 100 or 1000, you need to think about which number it is closest to on the number line. Take the number 3475...

3400 3410 3420 3430 3440 3450 3460 3470 3480 3490 **3500**
3475

3475 to the nearest 10 is 3480

3475 to the nearest 100 is 3500

3475 to the nearest 1000 is 3000

> **3475** is half way between **3470** and **3480** – if it is halfway or over you round up!

> If it is under halfway, round down.

Examples

1. Belvedere Rovers had 3762 fans at their last football match. Give this number to the nearest 10, 100 and 1000.

   Looking at the tens, 3762 is between 3760 and 3770. It is nearer to 3760 so...
   3762 to the nearest 10 is 3760

   Looking at the hundreds, 3762 is between 3700 and 3800. It is nearer to 3800 so...
   3762 to the nearest 100 is 3800

   Looking at the thousands, 3762 is between 3000 and 4000. It is nearer to 4000 so...
   3762 to the nearest 1000 is 4000

2. A girl has 235 books in her collection. Give this number to the nearest 10 and 100.

   Looking at the tens, 235 is between 230 and 240. It is nearer to 240 so...
   235 to the nearest 10 is 240

   > Always round a 5 up!

   Looking at the hundreds, 235 is between 200 and 300. It is nearer to 200 so...
   235 to the nearest 100 is 200

Now try these...

1. Round the following numbers to the nearest 10:
   a) 17   **b)** 29   **c)** 31
   d) 45   **e)** 6   **f)** 83

2. Round the following numbers to the nearest 100:
   a) 132   **b)** 845   **c)** 1555
   d) 692   **e)** 5124   **f)** 444

3. Round the following numbers to the nearest 10, 100 and 1000:
   a) 2834   **b)** 764   **c)** 5224
   d) 6450   **e)** 4725   **f)** 4938

Rounding Numbers

You need to know...

- **how to round numbers to a given number of decimal places**
- **how to round a number to a given number of significant figures.**

Numbers containing decimals can be rounded to a given number of **decimal places (d.p.)**. Decimal places are counted from the decimal point. For example, numbers with one decimal place have one digit after the decimal point, numbers with two decimal places have two digits after the decimal point etc.

To round a number in this way, you need to look at the digit that appears directly after the decimal place you are rounding to. If that digit is **5 or more** (i.e. 5, 6, 7, 8 or 9) you round up.

The same rule applies if you are rounding to a given number of **significant figures (s.f.)**.

The first significant figure in a number is the first digit that is not a zero. All the digits that come after this one are counted as significant figures even if they are zeros.

Examples

1. Round the following numbers to 3 d.p., 2 d.p. and 1 d.p.

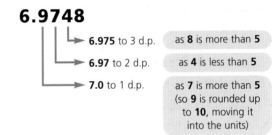

15.3642
- **15.364** to 3 d.p. — as **2** is less than **5**
- **15.36** to 2 d.p. — as **4** is less than **5**
- **15.4** to 1 d.p. — as **6** is more than **5**

6.9748
- **6.975** to 3 d.p. — as **8** is more than **5**
- **6.97** to 2 d.p. — as **4** is less than **5**
- **7.0** to 1 d.p. — as **7** is more than **5** (so **9** is rounded up to **10**, moving it into the units)

2. Round the following numbers to 3 s.f., 2 s.f. and 1 s.f.

0.1453
- **0.145** to 3 s.f. — as **3** is less than **5**
- **0.15** to 2 s.f. — as you round up **5**
- **0.1** to 1 s.f. — as **4** is less than **5**

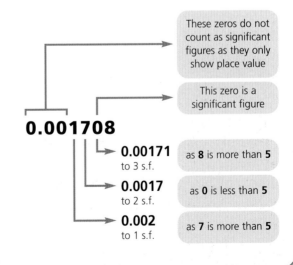

These zeros do not count as significant figures as they only show place value

This zero is a significant figure

0.001708
- **0.00171** to 3 s.f. — as **8** is more than **5**
- **0.0017** to 2 s.f. — as **0** is less than **5**
- **0.002** to 1 s.f. — as **7** is more than **5**

Now try these...

1. Round these to the given number of decimal places:
   a) 5.37 to 1 d.p.
   b) 18.015 to 2 d.p. and 1 d.p.
   c) 37.519 to 2 d.p. and 1 d.p.
   d) 0.0749 to 3 d.p., 2 d.p. and 1 d.p.

2. Round these to the given number of significant figures:
   a) 0.1259 to 1 s.f., 2 s.f. and 3 s.f.
   b) 12.05 to 1 s.f., 2 s.f. and 3 s.f.
   c) 67 029 to 1 s.f., 2 s.f., 3 s.f. and 4 s.f.
   d) 0.0000185 to 1 s.f., 2 s.f. and 3 s.f.

Calculator Examples

It is possible for calculators to unexpectedly give you an incorrect or inaccurate answer, so it is important that you can spot problems and mistakes when they occur.

1 Use your calculator to find 5 ÷ 6 x 3 x 2

You should get ☐ 5 but some calculators may show 4.9999998 . You have to interpret the display as meaning **5**.

2 Use your calculator to find the cost of 2 sports bags at £18.60 each.

You should get ☐ 37.2 . However, because we are dealing with money, you need to remember to write the answer as **£37.20**.

i You need to know...

- **how to estimate the answers to simple calculations**
- **how to check answers are reasonable by looking at the size of the numbers involved**
- **how to use your knowledge of maths to check results obtained using a calculator.**

Approximations give you a rough idea of what the answer to a calculation will be. Such an answer is often called an **estimate**.

To find an approximate answer to a calculation, you start by rounding the numbers and then do the maths.

You can use an approximation to check that the answer to a calculation is the size you would expect it to be. For example, if you were calculating 64 x 3 and got 1812, you could spot your mistake because you know 60 x 3 = 180 so your answer should be about that size (the correct answer is 192).

Examples

1 Find an approximate answer to 23 x 37.

23 ≈ 20 and **37 ≈ 40**

≈ means **approximately equal to**

20 x 40 = 800 so, **23 x 37 ≈ 800**

23 x 37 = 851 so our estimate is quite good

2 Estimate the value of $\frac{67 - 18}{8.9}$.

$$\frac{67 - 18}{8.9} ≈ \frac{70 - 20}{10} = \frac{50}{10} = 5$$

The correct answer is **5.5** to 1 d.p.

? Now try these...

1 Give sensible approximations for the following numbers:

a) 56   b) 7.9   c) 172   d) 534   e) 2279

2 Estimate the value of 17 x 32. Then use a calculator to find the exact answer.

3 Estimate the value of $\frac{176 + 23}{18.2}$. Then see how accurate your estimate is by finding the exact value.

4 Use approximation to say whether these calculations look reasonable or wrong:

a) 13 x 59 = 767

b) 46 x 105 = 48 030

c) 78 − 22 + 156 = 3354

d) 385 ÷ 23 = 17

e) 23 x 49 = 11 127

Checking Answers

ℹ You need to know...

- **how to check your answers by applying inverse operations or estimating using approximations.**

You can check your answers to calculations in two ways.

The first method is to use approximation to check that your answer looks reasonable i.e. that it is about the size you would expect it to be, as shown on the facing page.

When performing calculations involving lots of numbers, you can make a quick estimate by rounding each value to 1 s.f. This will give you the 'order of magnitude' of your expected answer i.e. it will tell you whether your answer will be in the tens, hundreds, thousands, etc. or whether it will be a decimal.

If your answer seems reasonable, you can then go on to check it for accuracy. To do this, start with your answer and work backwards through the calculation using inverse operations i.e. reversing the maths (see p.9). If your answer is correct, you should end up with the number you first started with.

Examples

1. What order of magnitude would you expect for the answer to this calculation?

$$\frac{152 \times 37}{8}$$

Round all the numbers involved to 1 s.f.

$$\frac{200 \times 40}{10} = \frac{80\,000}{10} = 800$$

So, the answer will be in the high hundreds! (The correct answer is 703).

2. Rachael goes shopping and buys the following items:

1 skirt at £6.99
2 tops at £3.75 each
1 pair of flip flops at £2.99

She pays with a £20 note and is given £1.52 change. Use estimation and inverse operations to check whether she has been given the correct change.

By estimation...
**£20 − £7 − £4 − £4 − £3 = £2
She has received roughly the right amount of change.**

Using inverse operations...
**£1.52 + £2.99 + £3.75 + £3.75 + £6.99
= £19.00
She has been short-changed by £1.**

❓ Now try these...

1. What order of magnitude would you expect for the answer to each of these calculations?
   a) 29 × 11
   b) 69 + 78 − 50
   c) $\dfrac{1000}{250}$
   d) $\dfrac{47 \times 120}{96}$

2. Check the following calculations by estimation and then for accuracy.
   a) 13 + 29 + 43 = 82
   b) 9.06 + 11.58 + 7.23 + 13.86 = 41.73
   c) $\dfrac{31 - 182}{57} = 26.5$
   d) $\dfrac{31 + 182}{57} = 3.74$

i You need to know...

- **the different roles played by letter symbols in algebra**
- **the difference in meaning between the words equation, formula, identity and expression**
- **that the letter symbols in algebra obey the rules of arithmetic.**

Algebra is a special type of maths, which uses letters and symbols to represent numbers and values.

The letters in algebra obey the rules of arithmetic. For example, they can be added, subtracted, multiplied and divided in just the same way as numbers.

Because the multiplication sign (**x**) could easily be confused with the letter x in algebra, numbers and letters to be multiplied are simply written alongside each other (with no space in between), e.g. **ab** means **a x b** or **a times b**.

When a letter is multiplied by a number, the number is always written first,
e.g. **y x 3** is written **3y**, not **y3**.

A line is used to show where numbers and letters are to be divided, just like in a fraction,
e.g. $\frac{a}{b}$ means **a ÷ b** or **a divided by b**.

A combination of letters, numbers and/or mathematical operations (e.g. add, subtract, multiply, divide) is called an **expression**. Expressions *do not* have an equals (=) sign. The examples below are all expressions:

$$ab, \quad \frac{5xy}{z}, \quad 12mn - p + 4q$$

Examples

Use the different mathematical operations (+, −, x and ÷) to show what the expressions below mean.

1. **2a**   ... **2 x a** or **a + a**

2. **cd**   ... **c x d** or **d x c**

3. $\frac{x}{z}$ ... $x ÷ z$

4. **3m − n**   ... **(3 x m) − n**

5. **4pq**   ... **4 x p x q**

6. **a²**   ... **a x a**

7. **a³**   ... **a x a x a**

? Now try these...

1. Use the different mathematical operations (+, −, x and ÷) to show what the expressions below mean.

   a) $6x$ d) $3m + 4n$

   b) abc e) $6 − 3d + 2e$

   c) $\frac{pq}{r}$ f) $x^2 + y$

2. Re-write the following examples as algebraic expressions:

   a) $4 \times d$ d) $a + a + a + a$

   b) $7 \times e \times f$ e) $c + c + c − d$

   c) $g ÷ h$ f) $2 \times a + b$

Basic Algebra

An **equation** is formed when two expressions are joined together by an equals (=) sign. An equation *always* has an equals sign. It shows that one expression is exactly equal to the other.

In algebra, the letters in equations represent **definite unknown numbers**. These unknown numbers can be found by solving the equation (see p.44).

This is an equation: $x + 6 = 9$

> x is an unknown number   equals sign

Unlike an equation, the letters in an **identity** do not represent specific numbers – they can take **any value**.

This is an identity: $a + a = 2a$

You can replace a in this identity with any number and it will always be true.

A **formula** is a general rule e.g. the formula for the area of a rectangle is $A = L \times W$ (where **A** stands for area, **L** stands for length and **W** stands for width).

The letters in a formula represent **variables**. That means their values can change. For example, the formula for finding the area of a rectangle is always the same, although the measurements for length and width may change, e.g. one rectangle could have a length of 10cm and a width of 5cm, whilst another could have a length of 15m and a width of 3m.

Examples

Decide whether each of the examples below is an expression, an equation, an identity or a formula.

① $3d = d + d + d$

> $d + d + d$ is just another way of writing **3d**, so **d** could take any value and it would always be true.

This is an identity

② $3d + 11 - 2e$

> There is no equals sign.

This is an expression

③ $C = 3d$, where C = circumference of a circle and d = diameter

> We are told that **C** and **d** represent measurements for circumference and diameter, so they are variables.

This is a formula

④ $3d = 12$

> **3d** is equal to **12**, so **d** must have a definite value.

This is an equation

③ For each of the examples below, decide whether it is an expression, an equation, an identity or a formula.

a) $g - 5 = 15$
b) $2g - 2h = g - h + g - h$
c) $t = g - 5$, where t = time in New York and g = Greenwich Mean Time
d) $g - h + g - h$
e) $2 = g - h + g - h$
f) $2(g + h) = 2g + 2h$
g) $a + a + a + a + 3 = 4a + 3$

You need to know...

- **how to simplify expressions by collecting like terms.**

A **term** is one part of an expression, equation or identity. It may be a letter, a number or a combination of letters and numbers.

Here is an expression: $4x - xy - 6 + x^2$

$+4x$, $-xy$, -6 and $+x^2$ are all terms. Terms always include the + or - sign in front of them.

Like terms contain the same letters and powers. The numbers and signs do not have to be the same.

Here is another expression:
$4x - 6 + 2x + 5 + 3x^2 - x^2$

$+4x$ and $+2x$ are like terms because they both contain an x. $+3x^2$ and $-x^2$ are like terms because they both contain an x^2. -6 and $+5$ are like terms because they both contain numbers only.

Expressions may be simplified by collecting together all the like terms.

Examples

1. Simplify the following expression by collecting like terms.

   $4x + 6 + 2x - 4$

   First, rearrange the expression so like terms are next to each other. Remember the signs!

   $$4x + 2x + 6 - 4$$

   all the x terms   all the number terms

   Then, simplify the expression by carrying out the mathematical operations (e.g. add or subtract the like terms).

   $4x + 2x + 6 - 4 = 6x + 2$

2. Simplify the following expression by collecting like terms.

   $$8xy + 4x - x + 7 - 3xy + 3$$
   $$= 8xy - 3xy + 4x - x + 7 + 3$$
   $$= 5xy + 3x + 10$$

? Now try these...

Simplify these expressions

1. $a + b + a + b + a$
2. $2x + y - x + 2y$
3. $p + 2 + 3p + q - 1$
4. $2xy + 1 + 5xy$
5. $6 + 2v + 3w - v - w - 2$
6. $2x^2 + x^2 - x$
7. $2d^2 + e^2 - d^2 + 5e^2 + 6$
8. $4p + 2q^2 - q + 2p$
9. $9 + 21z + 3 + 22z^2 + 22z$

Basic Algebra

i You need to know...

- **how to simplify or transform an expression by multiplying out a single pair of brackets.**

A number or letter immediately in front of brackets means that everything inside the brackets must be multiplied by that number or letter.

In algebra, when multiplying with negative and positive numbers and letters, the rules are the same as in arithmetic (see p.11)

$$+ \times + = +$$
$$- \times - = +$$

If the signs are the **same**, the answer is positive.

$$+ \times - = -$$
$$- \times + = -$$

If they are **different**, the answer is negative.

When you have multiplied out the brackets, you may need to simplify the expression by collecting like terms (see p.42).

Examples

Multiply out the brackets and where possible simplify the following expressions.

1 $6(a + 1)$

$= 6 \times a + 6 \times 1$

$= 6a + 6$

> **a** and **1** must both be multiplied by 6

2 $8(2x + 4y - 3z)$

$= 8 \times 2x + 8 \times 4y + 8 \times -3z$

$= 16x + 32y - 24z$

3 $3(p + 2) + 2(p - 1)$

$= 3 \times p + 3 \times 2 + 2 \times p + 2 \times -1$

$= 3p + 6 + 2p - 2$

$= 3p + 2p + 6 - 2$

$= 5p + 4$

> Now simplify the expression by collecting like terms

4 $a(a + 3) + b(a - 4)$

$= a \times a + a \times 3 + b \times a + b \times -4$

$= a^2 + 3a + ab - 4b$

> Remember, $a \times a = a^2$

5 $4(x + 3) + y(z - 5)$

$= 4 \times x + 4 \times 3 + y \times z + y \times -5$

$= 4x + 12 + yz - 5y$

6 $3p(p + 6) + 4p(2p + 1)$

$= 3p \times p + 3p \times 6 + 4p \times 2p + 4p \times 1$

$= 3p^2 + 18p + 8p^2 + 4p$

$= 11p^2 + 22p$

? Now try these...

Multiply out the brackets and, where possible, simplify the following expressions:

1 $5(p + 4)$

2 $6(2x - 3)$

3 $x(x + y + 3)$

4 $a(a + b)$

5 $3x(2x + 5y - 9)$

6 $3(x + 2) + 2(x - 1)$

7 $a(2a + b) + b(2b + a)$

8 $2(a + b) + a(2b + c) + 2b(a + c)$

9 $2p(p - 3) + 3p(2p - 2)$

10 $5a(b + 2) - 3a(b - 2)$

11 $6(a + b + c) + 2(2a - 2b - 2c)$

12 $5(2 - 3x) + 7x$

13 $11(5 - 3x) - 9$

14 $10(3x - 4) - 9x$

15 $5(3 - 2x + 7)$

Examples

1 An apple and a 20g weight are balanced with a 50g weight and a 20g weight. What does the apple weigh?

To find the weight of the apple, remove the 20g weight. To keep the balance, you must remove the 20g weight from the other side too.

Now we can see that the apple must weigh **50g**. If **a** stands for the weight of the apple this can be written as an algebraic equation:

$$a + 20 = 70$$
$$a + 20 - 20 = 70 - 20$$
$$a = 50g$$

2 A cake and a 10g weight are balanced with four 10g weights. What does the cake weigh?

If **c** stands for the weight of the cake:
$$c + 10 = 40$$

To find the weight of the cake, take 10g from both sides.

$$c + 10 - 10 = 40 - 10$$
$$c = 30$$

So the cake weighs **30g**.

ⓘ You need to know...

- **how to solve simple equations by balancing both sides.**

To solve an equation you must reduce it to a single letter on one side and a number on the other. All the other bits need to be removed.

An **equation** has an equals sign, because the left side of the equation has the same value as the right side. The two sides of the equation are **balanced**, and must always stay balanced.

It helps to think of the equation as a set of weighing scales. If anything is removed from or added to just one side, the scales are no longer in balance. To keep the balance, whatever is done to one side of the scales must also be done to the other side. When you solve an equation, the same rule applies.

❓ Now try these...

1 Write and solve an equation for each of these examples:

a)    b)

2 Solve these equations by balancing them:

a) $x + 5 = 25$ c) $p + 22 = 48$

b) $y + 15 = 100$ d) $t + 36 = 50$

Algebraic Equations

ℹ️ You need to know...

- **how to solve linear equations using inverse operations**
- **how to solve equations using trial and improvement.**

To solve an equation, collect all the letters on one side and all the numbers on the other. Then, reduce it to a single letter and number e.g. $x = 6$. To do this, you need to use **inverse operations** (inverse means opposite):

> **+** and **−** are inverse operations
>
> **×** and **÷** are inverse operations

Inverse operations can be used to cancel out unwanted numbers, but you must always remember to keep the equation balanced. For example, if you add a number to one side, you must add it to the other side too.

You can check your answer by putting it into the original equation, replacing the letter term.

Trial and improvement is a method used to find an approximate solution to an equation. Start by estimating a solution. Try your estimate out by putting it into the equation, replacing the letter term – it will probably be too big or too small. Use the results of your first trial to make a second estimate, better than the first. Each estimate you try should be better than the last, bringing you closer to the solution. Keep going until you get an answer accurate enough for your purposes.

❓ Now try these...

1. Solve these equations:

   a) $2p - 3 = 5$

   b) $5(x + 6) = 80$

   c) $2(x - 4) + 3 = 23$

   d) $a + 5 = 3a - 3$

2. Use trial and improvement to solve these equations to 1 d.p.:

   a) $x^2 = 29$

   b) $x^2 = 109$

   c) $x^2 = 78$

   d) $x^2 = 7$

Examples

1 Solve the equation $x - 4 = 20$.

$$x - 4 = 20$$
$$x - \cancel{4} + \cancel{4} = 20 + 4$$
$$x = 24$$

Add **4** to both sides to leave x on its own (-4 + 4 = 0)

Now, do the maths to find the solution

Check your answer
24 − 4 = 20

2 Solve the equation $4(x - 2) = 20$.

$$4(x - 2) = 20$$
$$4x - 8 = 20$$
$$4x - \cancel{8} + \cancel{8} = 20 + 8$$
$$4x = 28$$
$$\frac{4x}{4} = \frac{28}{4}$$
$$x = 7$$

Multiply out brackets first

Get the letter term on its own

Reduce to a single letter and number

÷**4** is the inverse operation of ×**4**

Check your answer:
4(7 − 2) = 20

3 Use trial and improvement to solve the equation $x^2 = 18$ (to 2 decimal places).

First estimate: **4**
$4^2 = 16$ Too small

Second estimate: **5**
$5^2 = 25$ Too big

The value of x must lie between 4 and 5, so...

Third estimate: **4.5**
$4.5^2 = 20.25$ Too big

Keep improving your estimates until you get an answer that is close enough:

$4.2^2 = 17.64$ Too small
$4.3^2 = 18.49$ Too big
$4.25^2 = 18.0625$ Too big
$4.24^2 = 17.9776$ Closest

So, $x = 4.24$ (2 d.p.)

You need to know...

- **how to use algebra to solve problems**
- **how to try out different ideas when solving mathematical problems.**

You will often be asked to use your mathematical skills to solve a problem written in words rather than numbers. Algebra can be useful because it may help to simplify the problem.

To deal with a problem...

1. read the question carefully, twice
2. underline the important words and numbers
3. decide what you are being asked to do
4. decide what maths you need to use to find the answer
5. write an equation
6. solve the equation
7. write down your answer to the question
8. check your answer.

Problems can sometimes be solved by working backwards through the question using inverse operations.

Look at Example 2 alongside. Start with the result, which is 16. Then go back through the question one step at a time and at each step reverse the maths. So, subtract 4, which leaves 12, then divide by 3, which gives 4 (the unknown number).

? Now try these...

1. I think of a number. If I take 2 away from my number I get the answer 8. What was my number?
2. I think of a number. I multiply my number by 5, then add 2. The answer is 32. What was my number?
3. I think of a number. I multiply it by 4 and then add 7. The answer is 27. What was my number?
4. I think of a number. If I add 6 to the number I get the answer 14. What was my number?
5. I think of a number. If I halve my number I get the answer 15. What was my number?

Examples

1. I think of a <u>number</u>. If I add <u>9</u> to my number, I get the answer <u>12</u>. What was my number?

Underline the important bits and use them to write an equation:

Let **n** be the unknown number	$n + 9 = 12$
Solve the equation	$n + \cancel{9} - \cancel{9} = 12 - 9$
	$n = 3$
Then check	$n + 9 = 12$
	$3 + 9 = 12$
Write the answer	**The number was 3**
You would get the same answer working backwards	$12 - 9 = 3$

2. I think of a <u>number</u>. If I <u>multiply</u> the number <u>by 3</u> then <u>add</u> 4 I get the answer <u>16</u>. What was my number?

Let **n** be the unknown number	$n \times 3 + 4 = 16$
	$3n + 4 = 16$
Solve the equation	$3n + \cancel{4} - \cancel{4} = 16 - 4$
	$3n = 12$
	$\dfrac{3n}{\cancel{3}} = \dfrac{12}{3}$
	$n = 4$
Then check	$3n + 4 = 16$
	$3 \times 4 + 4 = 16$
	$12 + 4 = 16$
Write the answer	**The number was 4**
Or, worked backwards:	$\dfrac{16 - 4}{3} = 16$

6. I think of a number. If I double my number and add 3 I get 19. What was my number?
7. Three apples cost 60p. How much does one apple cost?

Solving Problems

- **how to form and solve linear equations.**

A linear equation is an equation in which the unknown value is represented by a single letter e.g. **x** or **n**. There is no power or root to complicate things.

Providing you are given enough information, forming a linear equation can help you to find all sorts of unknown values e.g. missing angles and side lengths in shapes.

To construct an equation, you need to follow the same basic steps outlined on p.46. In addition to the information you are given in the question you may also need to draw upon your own knowledge of maths.

For example, you could be given the sizes of two angles in a triangle and asked to find the missing one. To answer the question you need to know that the interior angles of a triangle always add up to 180° (see p.66).

Examples

1 John's dad weighs twice as much as John. Their combined weight is 153kg. How much does John's dad weigh?

If John's weight is **j**, his dad's weight is **2j**. Their combined weight is 153kg:

$$j + 2j = 153$$
$$3j = 153$$
$$j = \frac{153}{3}$$

This is John's weight $j = 51kg$

Remember, the question asks 'How much does John's dad weigh?'

$$\textbf{John's dad} = \textbf{2j}$$
$$= \textbf{2 x 51}$$
$$= \textbf{102kg}$$

2 In this rectangle, the length is three times the width. The perimeter of the rectangle is 24cm. Find the length of the rectangle.

It might help if you draw and label a rectangle.

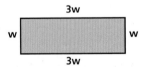

The perimeter (**P**) of a rectangle is found by adding all the sides together.

If **w** = width, then **length = 3w**	$P = w + 3w + w + 3w$
	$P = 8w$
We know **P = 24** so solve the equation	$8w = 24$
	$w = 3cm$

If **w = 3** then...	**length = 3w**
	length = 3 x 3
	length = 9cm

Then check
3 + 9 + 3 + 9 = 24

Write the answer   **The length is 9cm**

1 The angles of a triangle are d°, 2d° and 3d°. What is the size of each angle?

2 I think of a number. I add 9 to the number then divide the total by 3. The answer is 4. What was my number?

3 Karen is 6 years older than her brother. Their ages added together make 28. How old is Karen?

4 My garden is 5 metres narrower than my next-door neighbour's garden. Both gardens together are 45 metres wide. How wide is my garden?

5 Dan's mother is exactly three times older than Dan. The difference between their ages is 24 years. How old is Dan's mother?

ℹ️ You need to know...

- **how to construct simple formulae expressed in words and algebraic form.**

A formula can be written in words or as algebra, using letters to represent the variables (changeable quantities). Some mathematical formulae are well known

e.g. **area of a rectangle = length x width**
or **A = LW**

You can write a formula for any situation that involves a mathematical rule:

1. read the information you are given carefully
2. underline the important bits
3. describe what needs to be done in words
4. choose letters to represent the variables
5. write the formula, putting in the appropriate mathematical operations and an equals sign.

Examples

1. Jay earns £8 per hour. Write a formula for Jay's total earnings.

   For every hour that Jay works, he earns £8, so to get his total earnings we need to multiply the number of hours he works by £8.

   In words:
   Total earnings = 8 x hours worked

   Using algebra:
   **T stands for total earnings,
   H stands for hours worked**

   So **T = 8H**

2. Football teams get 3 points for a win and 1 point for a draw. Write a formula for the total points scored by a team during a season.

   The total points will be the number of games won multiplied by 3, plus the number of games drawn multiplied by 1.

   In words:
   Total points = 3 x wins + 1 x draws

   Using algebra:
   T stands for total points, W stands for games won, D stands for games drawn

   So **T = 3W + D**

❓ Now try these...

1. At the chip shop, fish costs £2 per portion and chips cost £1 per portion. Write a formula for the total cost of an order.
2. CDs cost £8 each and DVDs cost £15 each. Write a formula for the total cost of buying some CDs and DVDs.
3. A garage pays each of its staff £80 per day. Write a formula for the garage's total wage bill per day.
4. Postage stamps are sold by a shop in books of 12. Write a formula for the total number of stamps bought by a customer.
5. James earns £200 per week selling cars. He also earns a bonus of £50 for every car he sells. Write a formula for James's total earnings in one week.

Formulae

You need to know...

- **how to construct and use simple formulae expressed using algebra.**

To construct a formula using algebra you first need to pick out the mathematical bits of the question. Once you know how the formula is to be used, you can start to put it together.

1 Write down the letters you will use for each **variable** – it helps to use obvious ones, like **C** for cost.

2 Write down the letter you are using for the **final answer or total**, followed by an equals sign.

3 Use the information from the question to build your formula – what maths do you need to use?

4 Make sure all the values used in the formula are in the **same units**, for example, you cannot have both **£** and **p** in the same formula.

5 When you have written the formula, check that the algebra you have used is correct, e.g. **0.2d** not **d0.2**.

To use a formula, you need to substitute (see p.50) the appropriate values into the equation and solve it.

Examples

1 A taxi company makes a fixed charge of £2.40 per journey plus 20p per kilometre.

a) Write a formula for the total cost of the journey.

> Let **C** stand for the total cost and **d** stand for the distance in kilometres.

C = 0.2d + 2.40

> This is the price per km (20p = £0.20) x distance travelled + fixed charge

b) What is the cost of a journey of 5km?

C = 0.2d + 2.40 when **d = 5km**
C = (0.2 x 5) + 2.40
C = 1 + 2.40 = £3.40

2 Books bought from an internet company cost £4.99 each. The delivery charge is an extra £2.99 per order.

a) Write a formula for the total cost of an order.

> Let **C** stand for the total cost and **b** stand for the number of books ordered.

C = 4.99b + 2.99

b) What is the total cost of 10 books?

if **b = 10**...
C = (4.99 x 10) + 2.99
C = 49.90 + 2.99
C = £52.89

Now try these...

1 At the cinema, an adult ticket costs £7 and a child ticket costs £2.50.
   a) Write a formula for the cost of a group visit to the cinema.
   b) What will be the cost of a cinema trip for 6 adults and 2 children?

2 Kevin is a salesperson. For every journey, he can claim a fixed amount of £10 for meals plus 40p per mile for travel expenses.
   a) Write a formula for the total amount of expenses claimed for every journey.
   b) How much can Kevin claim for a journey of 120 miles?

Examples

1 Find the value of $x - 5$ when $x = 9$.

$$x - 5 =$$
$$9 - 5 = 4$$

> Replace the x with the value for x, which is **9**

2 Find the value of $6a$ when $a = 2$.

$$6a =$$
$$6 \times 2 = 12$$

> **6a = 6 x a**. Replace the **a** with 2, so...

3 Find the value of $s + t$ when $s = 3$ and $t = 2$.

$$s + t =$$
$$3 + 2 = 5$$

4 The area of a rectangle is found using the formula A = L x W. Find A when L = 8cm and W = 3cm.

$$A = L \times W$$
$$= 8cm \times 3cm$$
$$= 24cm^2$$

> Don't forget the units!

5 A formula for the perimeter of a square is P = 4s, when s stands for the length of the side of the square. Find the perimeter of a square when the length of the side is 5cm.

$$P = 4s$$
$$= 4 \times 5 = 20cm$$

---

i You need to know...

- **how to find the value of an expression or formula by substituting.**

In team sports, the **substitute** is the player who is sent on to replace another member of the team. In maths, **substitution** is used to replace letters with numbers so that the value of an expression or formula can be worked out.

There are some important rules to remember:

- a number and a letter written together with no sign in between means they are multiplied together, so **3c** means **3 x c**, and **5ab** means **5 x a x b**
- in algebra, when you substitute values, the same rules apply as in normal arithmetic so do brackets first, then multiply and divide, and lastly add and subtract (see p.33).

When you are substituting...

1 write down the complete expression or formula
2 write it out again, substituting the given values into the right places
3 do the working out
4 write down the final answer.

? Now try these...

1 Use the formula for the area of a rectangle in Example 4 above to find A when L = 9cm and W = 2cm.

2 Use the formula for the perimeter of a square in Example 5 above, to find P when s = 8cm.

3 Find the values of these expressions when a = 1, b = 2, and c = 3

a) a + b + c
b) 2a + b
c) 2b + 2c
d) a + b – c
e) 3c – b
f) abc
g) 3bc + a
h) 2b – a

Substitution

You need to know...

- **how to find the value of an expression or formula by substituting.**

There are two particular mathematical topics where you will be expected to find a value by substituting: using a formula and making a table of values for a linear graph.

A **formula** usually relates to a real life situation that involves mathematical rules. You may be given a special formula, such as the one for changing between Fahrenheit and Celsius, and be asked to use it.

When you are drawing the graph of an equation (see p.58), it helps to begin by making a **table of values**. This makes it easier to see the pairs of coordinates that are needed to plot the graph. You may need to choose values of x, and then substitute them into the equation to work out the corresponding values of y.

Now try these...

1. Use the formula in Example 1 to change 23°C to °F.
2. The recommended time to cook turkey is 35 minutes per kilogram plus an extra 20 minutes. Write a formula for the time to cook a turkey and use it to find the time to cook a 5kg turkey.
3. In science, Satvinder is using the formula $v = u + at$. In one experiment she finds that $u = 30$, $a = -3$ and $t = 6$. Use the formula to calculate v.
4. Complete this table of values for the equation $y = 3x + 9$.

x	-2	-1	0	1	2
$y = 3x + 9$					

Examples

1. The formula to change a temperature from degrees Celsius (°C) to degrees Fahrenheit (°F) is:

$$F = \frac{9C}{5} + 32$$

Find the value of 16°C in °F.

$$F = \frac{9C}{5} + 32$$

$$= \frac{9 \times 16}{5} + 32$$

$$= \frac{144}{5} + 32$$

$$= 28.8 + 32 = 60.8°F$$

2. The cost of hiring a dinghy is £4 per hour plus a fixed charge of £5. Write a formula for the total cost of hiring a dinghy, and use the formula to find the cost of hiring it for 3 hours.

C = 4h + 5

Let **C** stand for cost and **h** stand for number of hours.

When h = 3...

C = 4 x 3 + 5

C = 12 + 5 = £17

3. Complete the table of values for $y = 4x - 5$

x	-2	-1	0
$y = 4x - 5$			

When $x = -2$,
$y = 4x - 5 = (4 \times -2) - 5 = -8 - 5 = -13$
When $x = -1$,
$y = 4x - 5 = (4 \times -1) - 5 = -4 - 5 = -9$
When $x = 0$,
$y = 4x - 5 = (4 \times 0) - 5 = 0 - 5 = -5$

x	-2	-1	0
$y = 4x - 5$	-13	-9	-5

ⓘ You need to know...

- **how to recognise and describe simple number patterns.**

A **number pattern** is usually written as a string of numbers that are connected by a rule. A number pattern is sometimes called a **sequence**. Each number in the pattern is called a **term**, so the first number in the string is the 1st term, the second number is the 2nd term, etc.

Some sequences are easy to spot, such as even and odd numbers. Even number sequences and odd number sequences have the same rule – 'add two to the previous term' – but the sequences are different because the 1st term is different.

To describe a number pattern...
1. write down the sequence
2. find the difference between each term, this will tell you what type of rule it is:
   - difference **increases** by the **same** amount each time = **add**
   - difference **increases** by a **different** amount each time = **multiply**
   - difference **decreases** by the **same** amount each time = **subtract**
   - difference **decreases** by a **different** amount each time = **divide**
3. if the rule is multiply or divide, work out what number you must multiply or divide by
4. write down the rule.

? Now try these...

Find the rules for these number patterns...
1. 6, 12, 18, 24...
2. 100, 90, 80, 70...
3. 10 000, 1000, 100, 10...
4. 5, 10, 20, 40...
5. 1, 4, 16, 64...
6. 450, 400, 350, 300...
7. 32, 16, 8, 4...
8. 12, 24, 36, 48...

Examples

Find the rules for the following number patterns:

They are all even numbers.
The rule is: add 2 to the previous term.

They are all odd numbers.
The rule is: add 2 to the previous term.

The terms are decreasing so it must be a subtract or divide rule.
The rule is: subtract 3 from the previous term.

The terms are increasing so it must be an add or multiply rule. The difference changes each time so it must be multiply.
2 x 2 = 4, 2 x 4 = 8, 2 x 8 = 16...
The rule is: multiply the previous term by 2.

The terms are decreasing so it must be a subtract or divide rule. The difference changes each time so it must be divide.
120 ÷ 2 = 60, 60 ÷ 2 = 30, 30 ÷ 2 = 15.
The rule is: divide the previous term by 2.

Number Patterns

ℹ You need to know...

- **how to recognise and describe sequences**
- **how to continue a sequence using a rule.**

Once you know the rule for a sequence, you can use the rule to continue the sequence in either direction. You can also fill in any missing terms in the sequence. Remember that to describe a sequence fully, you need to know the rule, the value of the first term and the number of terms in the sequence.

To write down a sequence using a rule...
1 write down the first term
2 use the rule to generate the next term
3 continue to use the rule until you have the correct number of terms.

To fill in missing terms in a sequence...
1 write down the sequence, including the spaces for missing terms
2 use the given terms to find the rule for the sequence (remember, if you work backwards through the sequence, you need to use the opposite operation)
3 use the rule to find the missing terms.

Examples

1 The 1st term of a sequence is 8 and the rule is 'subtract 1 from the previous term'. Write down the first five terms:

8 – 1 = 7, 7 – 1 = 6, 6 – 1 = 5, 5 – 1 = 4
The sequence is: 8, 7, 6, 5, 4

2 The 1st term of a sequence is 2 and the rule is 'multiply the previous term by 6'. Write down the first four terms:

2 x 6 = 12, 12 x 6 = 72, 72 x 6 = 432
The sequence is: 2, 12, 72, 432

3 Find the missing terms in this sequence:
2, ___ , 12, 17, ___

The difference between **12** and **17** is **5**.
2 + 5 = 7 and **12 – 5 = 7** so the rule must be 'add 5 to the previous term'.
The sequence is: 2, 7, 12, 17, 22

4 Find the missing terms in this sequence:
___ , 6, ___ , 24, 48

The terms are increasing in value so the rule must be add or multiply.
24 + 24 = 48, so the rule is either 'add 24', or 'x 2'. **6 + 24 = 30**, but **24 – 24 = 0** so the rule must be 'multiply the previous term by 2'. To find the first term, work backwards from 6, using the opposite of 'x 2' which is '÷ 2'. So **6 ÷ 2 = 3**.
The sequence is: 3, 6, 12, 24, 48

❓ Now try these...

1 Write down the first five terms of each sequence:
   a) The first term is 75, the rule is 'subtract 8 from the previous term'.
   b) The first term is 1, the rule is 'multiply the previous term by 7'.

2 Find the missing terms in each sequence:
   a) 1, 5, ___ , ___ , 17,
   b) ___ , 6, 18, ___ , 162,
   c) ___ , 400, ___ , 4, 0.4,
   d) 180, ___ , ___ , 120, ___ ,

You need to know...

- **how to find a number pattern or sequence from a diagram.**

Number patterns can be formed by making a sequence of shapes. Shapes, matches or dots can all be used to make a sequence. The number pattern can then be made by counting the number of shapes, sides, corners or dots.

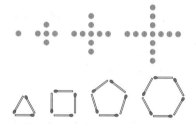

To find a number pattern in a sequence of shapes, look at the diagrams to see how they have been put together – what shapes have been used? Make sure you read the question carefully – you may be asked to draw the next shape in the sequence, to use a rule to work out the next number in the sequence or to find a rule for the sequence (see p.52).

? Now try these...

This sequence of hexagons is made from matches.

1 Draw the next shape in the sequence.

2 **a)** How many hexagons are in each shape?
b) Write down the sequence for the number of hexagons.
c) Write down a rule for the number of hexagons.
d) How many hexagons would there be in the 10th shape?

3 **a)** How many matches are needed for each shape?
b) Write down the sequence for the number of matches.
c) Write down a rule for the sequence.
d) How many matches would be needed for the 10th shape?

Examples

1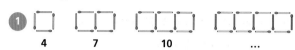

This sequence has been made with matches. The number of matches used to make each diagram is written beneath it.

a) How many matches are needed for the 4th shape?

Count the number of matches – there are **13 in the 4th shape**.

b) Write down a rule for the sequence.

The sequence is:

The rule is: add 3 to the previous term.

2 Look at this sequence…

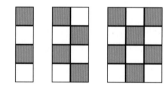

a) Draw the 4th shape in the sequence.

b) Write a rule for the number of red squares in the shapes.

The number pattern for the red squares is:

The rule is: add 2 to the previous term.

c) Without drawing the shape, how many red squares will there be in the 10th shape?

The 1st shape has 2 red squares, the 2nd has 4 etc. so the 10th shape will have **20 red squares**.

Number Patterns

You need to know...

- **how to find and describe the nth term of a linear sequence.**

A **linear sequence** is a number sequence in which the terms increase or decrease by the same amount each time i.e. they follow a simple add or subtract rule.

A formula can be used to calculate the value of any term in a linear sequence. In this formula **n** is used to represent the position of the term in the sequence (1st, 2nd, 3rd etc.) so this method is called finding the **nth term**.

The formula takes the form: **nth term = an + b**

To use the formula to find the nth term of a particular sequence...

1. Number each term in the sequence. These numbers are values for **n**.

2. Find the difference between the terms in the sequence. If the numbers in the sequence increase, it will be a positive number. If the numbers decrease, it will be a negative number. This number is your value for **a**.

3. Calculate the value of **an** (a x n) for each given term in the sequence and write your answer directly beneath that term.

4. Now subtract the bottom number (your value for an) from the top number (the term). Write down your answer, including the + or – sign. The answer should be the same for each term. This number is your value for **b**.

5. Substitute your values for a and b into the formula **nth term = an + b**.

6. To find the value of a specific term in the sequence, substitute the number of the term for n in the formula.

Example

Here is a sequence:

7   11   15   19   23

a) Find a formula for the nth term of the sequence.

Number the terms. These numbers are values for **n**.

$$\begin{array}{ccccc} 1 & 2 & 3 & 4 & 5 \\ 7 & 11 & 15 & 19 & 23 \end{array}$$

The difference between each terms is **+4**. This is your value for **a**.

$+4 \quad +4 \quad +4 \quad +4$

So, the formula starts with **4n**. Calculate **4n** for each term.

4   8   12   16   20

Subtract these numbers from the original sequence to find the value for **b**, e.g. **7 - 4 = +3**

$+3 \quad +3 \quad +3 \quad +3 \quad +3$

The formula for the nth term is **4n + 3**

b) What will be the 100th term in the sequence?

$$\text{nth term} = 4n + 3$$
$$= 4 \times 100 + 3$$
$$= 400 + 3 = 403$$

Substitute **100** for the **n** in the formula

c) The number 111 is in the sequence, which term is it?

$$4n + 3 = \text{nth term}$$
$$4n + 3 = 111$$
$$4n + 3 - 3 = 111 - 3$$
$$4n = 108$$
$$\frac{4n}{4} = \frac{108}{4}$$
$$n = 27$$

If 111 is in the sequence, then...

Solve the equation

So **111 is the 27th term.**

Now try these...

For each of these sequences...
a) find the nth term
b) use the formula to find the 50th term.

1. 5, 8, 11, 14, 17
2. -27, -25, -23, -21, -19
3. 1, 1.5, 2, 2.5, 3
4. In ③ the number 25.5 appears later in the sequence. Which term is it?

(i) You need to know...

- **how to use and understand coordinates in the first quadrant.**

Coordinates are pairs of numbers that are used to describe the position of a point on a square grid. The grid has a horizontal axis called the **x-axis** and a vertical axis called the **y-axis**. The axes are numbered from 0, going from left to right and from bottom to top. The point where the x and y axes cross is called the **origin**. The coordinates of the origin are (0,0).

Coordinates are always written with the x value first, followed by the y value. They are put in brackets and are separated by a comma, i.e. **(x ,y)**. To find a point using coordinates, always go along the x-axis first, then up the y-axis.

Examples

1 Look at the graph below and write down the coordinates of...

a) A   **b)** B   **c)** C   **d)** D.

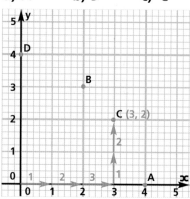

a) A (4,0) **b)** B (2,3) **c)** C (3,2) **d)** D (0,4)

2 Draw a graph with x and y axes numbered from 0 to 5. On your graph, mark the following points and label them as instructed...

a) P (1,1) **b)** Q (2,3) **c)** R (4,1) **d)** S (5,4)

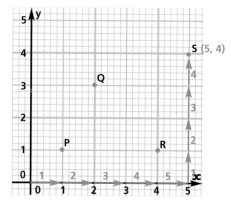

(?) Now try these...

1 On graph paper, draw and label x and y axes from 0 to 10.
On your graph, plot and label these points:
A (6,7), B (2,4), C (3,1), D (10,0), and E (0,10).
Join points D and E with a straight line. Mark a point F exactly halfway between D and E. What are the coordinates of point F?

2 a) Write down the coordinates of all the points marked on the graph alongside.

b) What do you notice about the coordinates of the points on the line PQR and on the line STU?

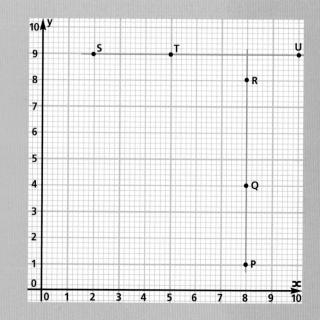

Coordinates

i You need to know...

- **how to use and understand coordinates in all four quadrants.**

The x and y axes of a graph can be extended beyond the origin. If this is done, the axes of the graph divide the space into four parts. These parts are called **quadrants**. Each quadrant has different properties, which are shown in the coordinates of the point.

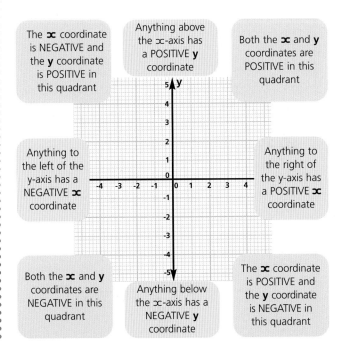

The x coordinate is NEGATIVE and the **y** coordinate is POSITIVE in this quadrant

Anything above the x-axis has a POSITIVE **y** coordinate

Both the x and **y** coordinates are POSITIVE in this quadrant

Anything to the left of the y-axis has a NEGATIVE x coordinate

Anything to the right of the y-axis has a POSITIVE x coordinate

Both the x and **y** coordinates are NEGATIVE in this quadrant

Anything below the x-axis has a NEGATIVE **y** coordinate

The x coordinate is POSITIVE and the **y** coordinate is NEGATIVE in this quadrant

To read and plot coordinates on a graph like this, follow the same rules as with all coordinates, i.e. x first (left or right from the origin), then y (up or down).

Example

Write down the coordinates of the points marked on the graph.

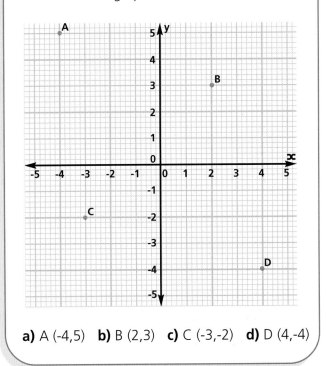

a) A (-4,5)   **b)** B (2,3)   **c)** C (-3,-2)   **d)** D (4,-4)

? Now try these...

1. On squared paper, draw and label x and y axes from −10 to 10.
   On your graph, plot and label these points:
   A (3,10), B (-7,-4), C (6,-6), and D (-2,3). Join points A and B with a straight line. What do you notice about point D?

2. Write down the coordinates of all the points marked on the graph alongside.

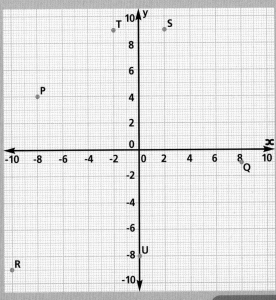

i You need to know...

- **the general features of straight line graphs.**

There are three types of straight line graph that you need to recognise and be able to sketch if necessary:

1. vertical lines
2. horizontal lines
3. the main diagonal lines.

The lines are easy to recognise by their equations. Equations in the form x = **a number** give **vertical** line graphs. The line will cross the x-axis at 'the number', and will never cross the y-axis.

Equations in the form **y = a number** give **horizontal** line graphs. The line will cross the y-axis at 'the number', and will never cross the x-axis.

There are two main **diagonal** lines, the graph of **y = x** goes **up** from left to right, and **y = -x** goes **down** from left to right.

When you are asked to sketch the graph of an equation, remember that it will not be an accurately plotted graph, but the lines must be in reasonable or sensible positions on the axes.

? Now try these...

1. On squared paper, draw unnumbered x and y axes. Sketch and label the graphs of...

a) y = 4

b) x = -2

c) y = x

d) x = 8

e) y = -x

f) x = -6

Label the coordinates of any points where your lines cross the x or y axes.

Examples

For each question draw separate axes and draw the graphs of the following lines...

1. **a)** x = 3

   b) x = -1

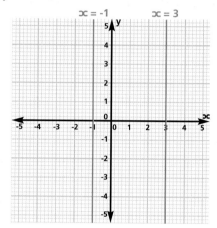

2. **a)** y = 5

   b) y = -4

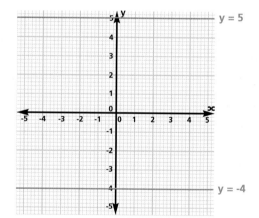

3. **a)** y = x

   b) y = -x

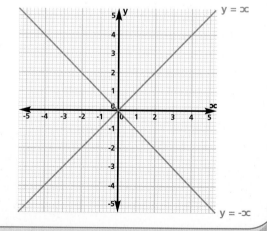

Graphs

You need to know...

- **how to use coordinates to plot the graphs of linear equations.**

If an equation is linear, i.e. there are no x^2 terms or other powers of x (see p.12), the graph of the equation will be a straight line.

Before you can draw an accurate graph of an equation, you need to produce a table of values. To do this, you will be given values of x from which to work out the values of y. Write down the equation and then substitute each given value of x from the table into the equation to find the corresponding y values (see p.50). Write the values of y into the correct positions in the table.

The table of values will provide pairs of x and y values that make up coordinates. Accurately plot each pair of coordinates on the graph, marking them with a cross or small dot. When all the points have been plotted, join them carefully with a ruler to form the graph – a straight line graph MUST be drawn with a ruler. When you join the points it will be obvious if any of them do not fit the straight line. If this occurs, these points must be wrong, so check your working and make sure that you have plotted each point correctly.

Example

Draw a table of values of x from -2 to 2 and use it to draw the graph of y = 2x + 3.

Substitute the values of x into the formula:

When x = -2, y = 2 x -2 + 3 = **-1**
When x = -1, y = 2 x -1 + 3 = **1**
When x = 0, y = 2 x 0 + 3 = **3**
When x = 1, y = 2 x 1 + 3 = **5**
When x = 2, y = 2 x 2 + 3 = **7**

x	-2	-1	0	1	2
y	-1	1	3	5	7

Now draw and label the graph using each pair of values as coordinates for the points.

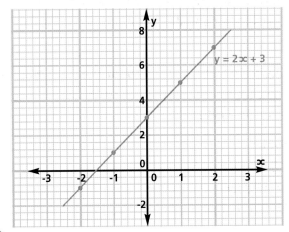

? Now try these...

1 Complete this table of values and use it to draw the graph of y = 3x – 4

x	-1	0	1	2	3
y					

2 Use values of x from -2 to 2 to make a table of values for the equation y = $\frac{1}{2}x$ + 5. Use your table of values to plot the graph of y = $\frac{1}{2}x$ + 5.

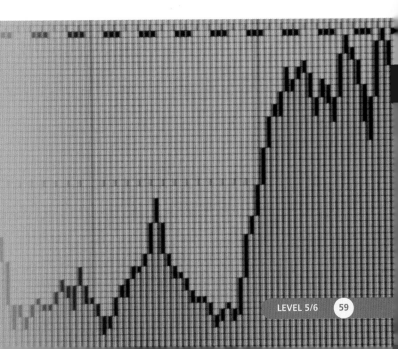

ℹ️ You need to know...

- **the metric and imperial measurements of length, mass and capacity**
- **how to convert measurements within the same system.**

Measurements can be made in **metric** or **imperial units**. You will have used mainly metric units but imperial units are still in common use.

Length

Metric units are millimetres (mm), centimetres (cm), metres (m) and kilometres (km).
Imperial units are inches (in.), feet (ft), yards (yds) and miles.

Metric	Imperial
10mm = 1cm	12 in. = 1 ft
100cm = 1m	3 ft = 1 yd
1000m = 1km	1760 yds = 1 mile

Mass

Metric units are milligrams (mg), grams (g), kilograms (kg) and tonnes.
Imperial units are ounces (oz), pounds (lb), stones (st.) and tons.

Metric	Imperial
1000mg = 1g	16 oz = 1 lb
1000g = 1kg	14 lbs = 1 st.
1000kg = 1 tonne	160 st. = 1 ton

Capacity / Volume

Metric units are millilitres (ml), centilitres (cl) and litres (l).
Imperial units are fluid ounces (fl oz), pints (pts) and gallons (gal.).

Metric	Imperial
10ml = 1cl	20 fl oz = 1 pt
100cl = 1l	8 pts = 1 gal.

Examples

1 Convert 25cm into mm and m.

$$1cm = 10mm$$
so 25cm = 25 × 10mm
$$= 250mm$$

$$100cm = 1m$$
so 25cm = 25 ÷ 100cm
$$= 0.25m$$

2 Convert 450kg into g and tonnes.

$$1kg = 1000g$$
so 450kg = 450 × 1000g
$$= 450\ 000g$$

$$1000kg = 1\ tonne$$
so 450kg = 450 ÷ 1000kg
$$= 0.45\ tonnes$$

3 Convert 75cl into ml and l.

$$1cl = 10ml$$
so 75cl = 75 × 10ml
$$= 750ml$$

$$100cl = 1l$$
so 75cl = 75 ÷ 100cl
$$= 0.75l$$

❓ Now try these...

1 Convert each of these to cm:
 a) 5m **b)** 1200mm **c)** 12.6m **d)** 9km

2 Convert each of these to kg:
 a) 1010g **b)** 3.3 tonnes **c)** 555g
 d) 1265 000mg

3 Convert each of these to l:
 a) 600ml **b)** 100cl **c)** 4400ml **d)** 80cl

4 How many ft in 15 yds?

5 How many oz in $7\frac{1}{4}$ lbs?

6 Convert 76 pints into gallons.

7 How many yards are there in 10 miles?

Metric and Imperial Units

ℹ You need to know...

- **the rough metric equivalents of imperial units still in daily use.**

The tables below give acceptable equivalent values for metric and imperial measurements. The symbol ≈ means 'approximately equal to'.

Length

1 inch ≈ 2.5cm
1 foot ≈ 30cm
1 yard ≈ 91cm
1 mile ≈ 1.6km
(Remember a 30cm ruler is about a foot long)

Mass

1 ounce ≈ 28g
1 pound ≈ 454g
1 stone ≈ 6.4kg
1 ton is a bit more than 1 tonne
(Remember that a bag of sugar weighs 1kg, which is about 2.2lbs)

Capacity

1 pint ≈ 0.6 litres
1 gallon ≈ 4.5 litres
(Remember: a litre of water is a pint and three quarters.)

Examples

1 Convert 35 miles into km.

1 mile ≈ 1.6km

so **35 miles ≈ 35 x 1.6 = 56km**

2 Convert 750g to pounds.

454g ≈ 1lb

so **750g ≈ 750 x 454 = 1.6lbs**

3 Convert 14 gallons to l.

1 gallon ≈ 4.5l

so **14 gallons ≈ 14 x 4.5 = 63l**

❓ Now try these...

1 Convert 75cm into inches.
2 Roughly how many ounces are there in 200g?
3 Convert 15l into gallons.
4 Roughly how many cm are there in $4\frac{1}{2}$ feet?
5 Convert 64kg into pounds.
6 Roughly how many pints are there in 3.6l?
7 Which is heavier: a tonne of feathers or a tonne of bricks?
8 Which is the longest distance to run: a marathon (26.2 miles) or 40km?

You need to know...

- **how to read and interpret number scales on a range of measuring instruments.**

You must be able to use measuring instruments such as weighing scales, pressure gauges and rulers. Some **scales** are more accurate than others and it is important to take time to understand what they are showing.

When reading a scale, you need to look at the divisions between the numbers and work out what each division represents.

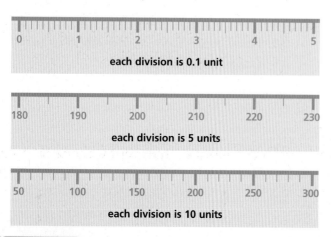

each division is 0.1 unit

each division is 5 units

each division is 10 units

Examples

1 What value is shown by each of the arrows?

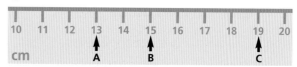

Arrow A shows 13cm
Arrow B shows 15cm
Arrow C shows 19cm

2 What value is shown by each of the arrows?

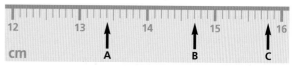

Arrow A shows 13.4cm
Arrow B shows 14.7cm
Arrow C shows 15.8cm

3 Estimate the values shown by the arrows on the scale.

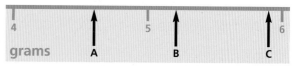

Arrow A shows about 4.6g
Arrow B shows about 5.2g
Arrow C shows about 5.9g

? Now try these...

1 Put these arrows on the scale:
  Arrow A at 14   Arrow B at 24
  Arrow C at 22   Arrow D at 17

2 Give the values shown by the arrows on the scale.

Measurement

You need to know...

- **how to read and interpret scales on a range of measuring equipment with appropriate accuracy.**

The divisions on these scales represent smaller numbers, so you can make more accurate readings.

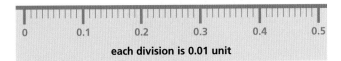

each division is 0.01 unit

When the indicator lies between two divisions, you can estimate a reading or round up depending on the level of accuracy you are asked for.

You could estimate the reading on these weighing scales as 1385g or give it as 1390g to the nearest 10g.

Examples

1 What value is shown by each of the arrows?

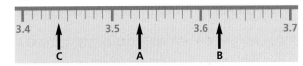

Arrow A shows 3.53
Arrow B shows 3.62
Arrow C shows 3.44

2 What value is shown by each of the arrows?

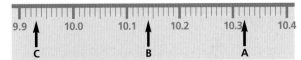

Arrow A shows 10.32
Arrow B shows 10.14
Arrow C shows 9.93

3 Estimate the values shown by the arrows on the scale.

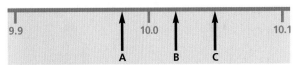

Arrow A shows about 9.98
Arrow B shows about 10.02
Arrow C shows about 10.05

Now try these...

1 Estimate the values shown by the arrows on the scales below.

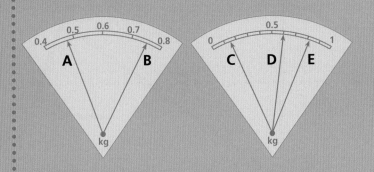

2 Put these arrows on the scale:
Arrow A at 7.9   Arrow B at 8.85
Arrow C at 5.65   Arrow D at 7.05

3 Give the values shown by the arrows on the scale.

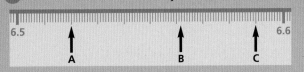

Measurement

You need to know...

- **how to make sensible estimates of a range of measures in relation to everyday situations.**

If you are asked to estimate a quantity or measurement, you need to apply some common sense.

Try to make comparisons with objects that you know the size of e.g. a standard ruler measures approximately 30cm and a bag of sugar weighs 1 kilogram.

Make sure you always use a sensible unit of measurement for your estimates.

For example, look at this book. You can see that the length of the book is roughly the same as the length of a ruler. Therefore, 30cm would be a good estimate.

Example

The tree is 10m tall. Estimate the heights of the other objects.

If you get a question like this in an exam, there won't be a scale alongside the drawing. However, you can sketch your own if it helps.

The pylon is about 25m tall.
The block of flats is about 20m tall.
The bird is flying at about 30m.
The helicopter is flying at about 35m.

Now try these...

1. Make sensible estimates for the following measures:
   a) the mass of a house brick.
   b) the height of your bedroom door.
   c) the amount of water in a window cleaner's bucket when it is full.
   d) the height of your school desk.
   e) the height of the worksurface in your kitchen at home.
   f) the diameter of a CD.

2. This line is 5cm long.

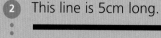

   Estimate the lengths of these lines.

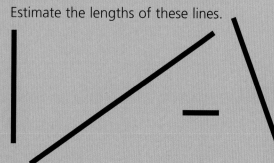

Angles

i You need to know...

- **how many degrees there are in a full turn, half turn and quarter turn**
- **how to identify acute, obtuse, reflex and right angles.**

An **angle** is a measure of rotation or turn. Degrees (°) are the unit of measurement used to describe angles.

There are **360°** in a full turn.

There are **180°** in a half turn.

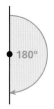

There are **90°** in a quarter turn. A quarter turn is also called a **right angle** and we used this symbol ⌐ to show a right angle in diagrams. (⌐ This is not a left angle!)

Angles between 0° and 90° are called **acute** angles.

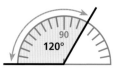
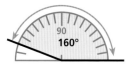

Angles between 90° and 180° are called **obtuse** angles.

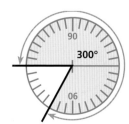
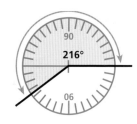

Angles between 180° and 360° are called **reflex** angles.

? Now try these...

1. Complete the following sentences:
   a) A 90° angle is known as a ....angle.
   b) An angle of 57° is an............................ angle.
   c) Obtuse angles are between ....° and ....°.
   d) A half turn is exactly..............°.

2. Are the following angles acute, obtuse or reflex?
   a) 320°   **f)** 123°
   b) 40°   **g)** 17°
   c) 91°   **h)** 279°
   d) 178°   **i)** 109°
   e) 311°   **j)** 359°

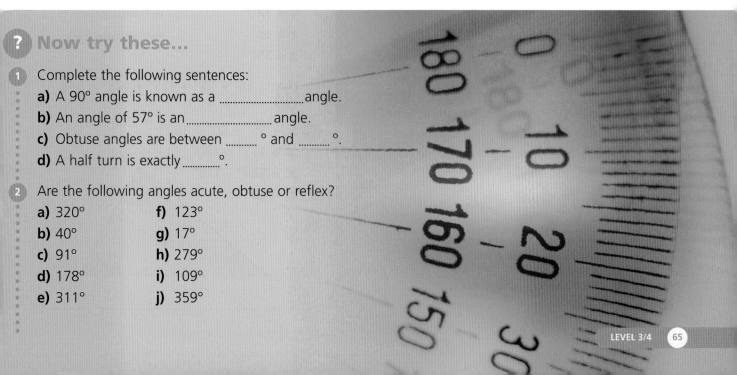

ⓘ You need to know...

- **the properties of angles on a straight line and at a point**
- **that the angles in a triangle add up to 180°.**

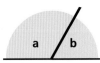

Angles on a straight line add up to 180°.

a + b = 180°

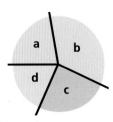

Angles at a point add up to 360°.

a + b + c + d = 360°

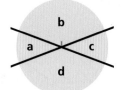

When two straight lines intersect (i.e. cross), the angles opposite each other are equal. **a = c** and **b = d**. These are called **vertically opposite angles**.

Notice also that:

$$\left.\begin{array}{l} \textbf{a + b = 180°} \\ \textbf{b + c = 180°} \\ \textbf{c + d = 180°} \\ \textbf{a + d = 180°} \end{array}\right\}$$ These are all angles on a straight line

and

a + b + c + d = 360° = the angles around a point.

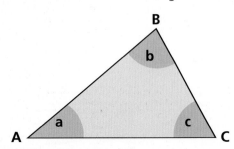

Angles in a triangle add up to 180°.

a + b + c = 180°

Examples

Work out the value of x in each of the following:

① $x + 30° = 180°$
$x = 180° - 30°$
$x = 150°$

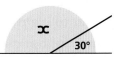

② $x + 65° + 90° = 180°$
$x + 155° = 180°$
$x = 180° - 155°$
$x = 25°$

③ $x + 62° + 80° = 360°$
$x + 142° = 360°$
$x = 360° - 142°$
$x = 218°$

④ Work out the values of x, y and z.

$x + 125° = 180°$
$x = 180° - 125°$ on a straight line
$x = 55°$
$y = 125°$ vertically opposite
$z = x$ vertically opposite
$z = 55°$

check: **55° + 55° + 125° + 125° = 360°**

⑤ $x + 55° + 60° = 180°$
$x + 115° = 180°$
$x = 180° - 115°$
$x = 65°$

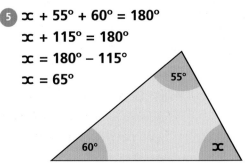

Angles

i You need to know...

- **the properties of corresponding, alternate and co-interior angles.**

When a straight line crosses two or more **parallel lines** it is called a **traversal** and new angles are created.

Alternate Angles

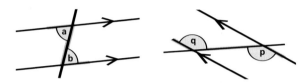

Alternate angles are always equal in size. Alternate angles can be easily spotted because they form a letter **Z** (although sometimes it may be reversed, **Ƨ**!!).

Corresponding Angles

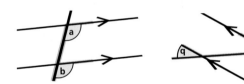

Corresponding angles are always equal in size. Corresponding angles can be easily spotted because they form a letter **F** (although sometimes it may be reversed, **Ⅎ**, or upside down **Ⴇ, Ⴃ**!!)

Co-Interior Angles

Co-interior angles always add up to 180°. Co-interior angles can be easily spotted because they form a letter **⊏** or **⊔** (although sometimes it may be reversed, **⊐** or **⊓**!!).
Co-interior angles are sometimes called 'supplementary' or 'allied' angles.

Example

Work out the value of each of the letters in the diagram.

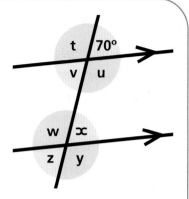

$t + 70° = 180°$	angles on a straight line
$t = 180° - 70°$	
$t = 110°$	
$u = t = 110°$	vertically opposite angles
$v = 70°$	vertically opposite angles
$w = u = 110°$	alternate angles
$x + u = 180°$	co-interior angles
$x + 110° = 180°$	
$x = 180° - 110°$	
$x = 70°$	
$y = w = 110°$	vertically opposite angles
$z = v = 70°$	corresponding angles

? Now try these...

Find the angles marked with letters.

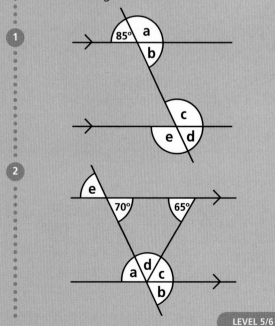

ℹ️ You need to know...

- **the properties of angles in quadrilaterals**
- **the properties of angles in polygons.**

Quadrilaterals

A quadrilateral is a shape with 4 sides. The **interior** angles in all **quadrilaterals** add up to 360°.

a + b + c + d = 360°

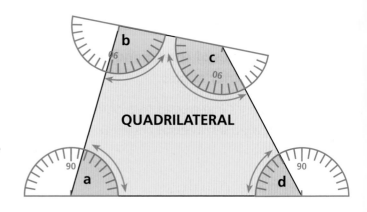

QUADRILATERAL

Polygons

A polygon is any shape with 3 or more sides. The **exterior** angles of any **polygon** add up to 360° (a full turn). In regular polygons, all exterior angles are equal. In regular polygons...

each exterior angle = $\frac{360}{n}$

(where n is the number of sides)

Notice also that for all polygons...

each interior angle + exterior angle = 180°

(angles on a straight line again!)

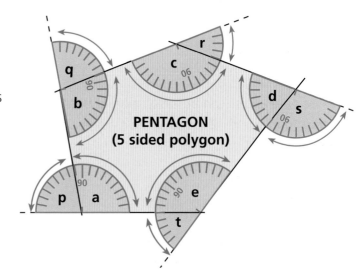

**PENTAGON
(5 sided polygon)**

Example

Calculate angles x and y in this regular octagon.

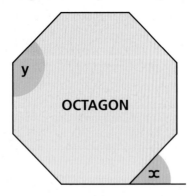

OCTAGON

An octagon has 8 sides, so...

$x = \frac{360°}{8} = 45°$

$x + y = 180°$

$45° + y = 180°$

$y = 180° - 45°$

$y = 135°$

❓ Now try these...

1 Calculate angle x in this quadrilateral.

85°

52°

2 Calculate angles x and y in this regular hexagon.

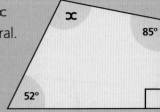

Angles

You need to know...

- **how to measure and draw angles.**

A protractor is used to measure angles. Most protractors are semi-circular and measure from 0° to 180°, but some are full circles and can go up to 360°. Many have two scales on them so they can be used to measure from the left or the right – this is where confusion can arise.

Example

How many degrees is this angle?

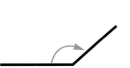 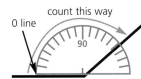

It is clearly an obtuse angle, i.e. it is between 90° and 180°. Place the protractor over the angle, making sure the cross is over the corner of the angle and zero is lined up with the baseline of the angle. Count up the scale until you get to the other line. **The angle measures 140°.**

To draw angles...

1. Draw a baseline about 5-6cm long. Mark a cross at one end.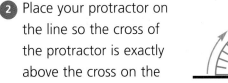

2. Place your protractor on the line so the cross of the protractor is exactly above the cross on the end of the line.

3. Count from zero to the angle you want and put a dot next to the number. Make sure you start at the correct zero line – it's the one that lies on your baseline.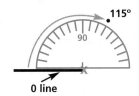

4. Remove the protractor and carefully join the dot to the centre of the cross. Finally, check the angle with your protractor.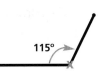

Now try these...

1. Measure these angles.

a)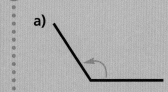

b)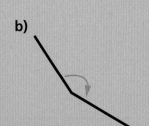

c)

d)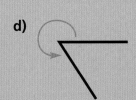

Hint: Measure the acute angle then subtract it from 360° to get the **reflex** angle.

2. Measure the angles in this triangle. Check that they add up to 180° - you may be 1° or 2° out!

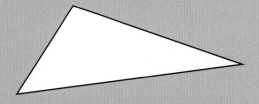

3. Draw the following angles...
   a) 35° b) 110° c) 147° d) 300°

Hint: what is 360° – 300°? Can you draw this angle more easily? Which part will you label '300°'?

i You need to know...

- **that one coordinate identifies a point on a number line**
- **that two coordinates identify a point on a plane.**

Coordinates are numbers used to describe the location of a point on a line or on a plane (a flat surface area).

To describe the location of a point on a line, you only need one coordinate. This is because lines only have one dimension (length) i.e. they are 1-D.

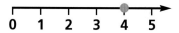

The location of this point is 4.

To describe the location of any point on a plane, you need two coordinates. This is because planes have two dimensions (length and width) i.e. they are 2-D.

Coordinates are written (**x, y**). x is the distance from 0 (the origin) along the x-axis. y is the distance from 0 along the y-axis (see p.56).

Example

Write down the coordinates of each letter on the grid.

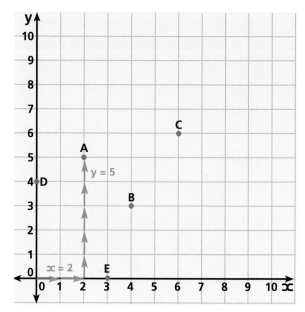

A = **(2,5)**
B = **(4,3)**
C = **(6,6)**
D = **(0,4)**
E = **(3,0)**

Remember, the x coordinate always comes first

? Now try these...

1. Draw axes (a grid) with x values from 0 to 10 and y values from 0 to 10. On your grid plot and label these points.

   A (5,6)
   B (4,9)
   C (8,0)
   D (10,2)
   E (3,3)
   F (0,5)
   G (7,4)
   H (5,9)

2. Write down the coordinates of the points marked with letters on the grid alongside.

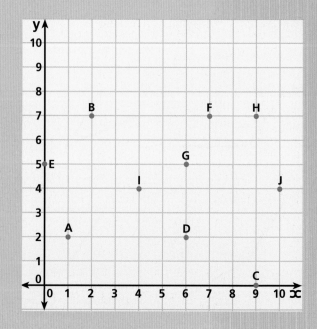

Coordinates

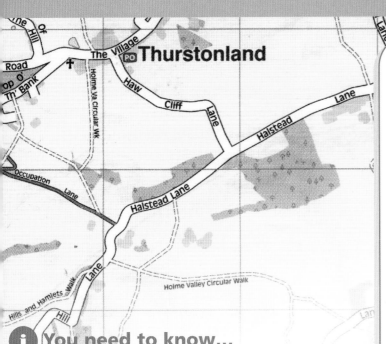

ℹ You need to know...

- **how to use axes and coordinates to identify points in all four quadrants.**

The x and y axes can be extended to include negative values. The coordinates are still written as (x,y), but care must be taken not to miss out or ignore any minus (-) signs. Extending the axes in this way gives us four 'sections' on the grid. These sections are called **quadrants** (see p.57).

Example

Write down the coordinates of the points marked with letters.

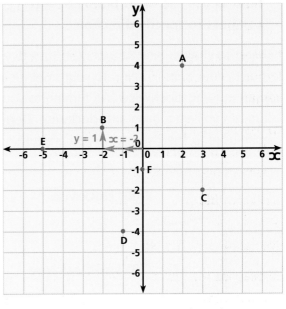

A = (2,4)	D = (-1,-4)
B = (-2,1)	E = (-5,0)
C = (3,-2)	F = (0,-1)

❓ Now try these...

1. Draw axes with x values from -8 to 8 and y values from -8 to 8. On your grid plot and label these points:

   A (-5,2)
   B (4,3)
   C (0,-6)
   D (-3,-3)
   E (7,3)
   F (-4,-1)
   G (-3,0)
   H (-6,8)

2. Write down the coordinates of the points marked with letters on the grid alongside.

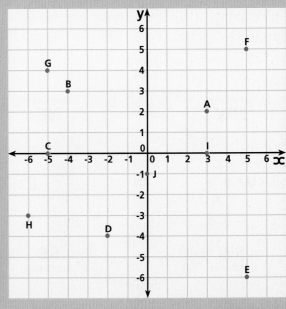

You need to know...

- **how to specify a change in direction using clockwise/anti-clockwise and degrees**
- **how to use the eight points of the compass to specify direction.**

In order to change direction you can turn to your left or to your right. Turning to your right means you are turning **clockwise** and turning to your left means you are turning **anti-clockwise**. **Degrees** can be used to specify how far you are turning.

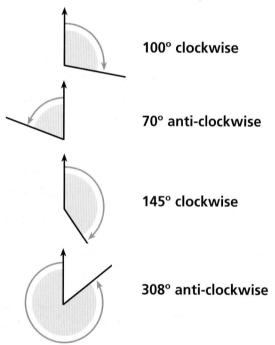

100° clockwise

70° anti-clockwise

145° clockwise

308° anti-clockwise

The eight points of the compass can also be used to specify direction.

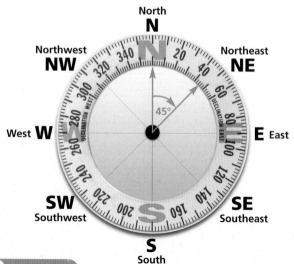

Example

If I am facing south and turn 135° clockwise, what is my new direction?

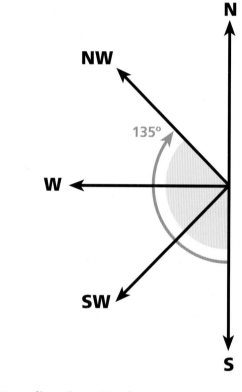

New direction: Northwest.

? Now try these...

1. What direction is 90° anti-clockwise from southeast?
2. A 280° turn clockwise is the same as what turn anti-clockwise?
3. How many degrees clockwise is it from southwest to east?
4. How many degrees anti-clockwise is it from northwest to northeast?
5. Start facing east. Turn 45° clockwise then 135° anti-clockwise. In which direction are you now facing?
6. Why doesn't it matter when turning through 180° whether you turn clockwise or anti-clockwise?

You need to know...

- **how to use and interpret scales on maps.**

All maps are drawn to a certain scale which enables you to measure a distance on the map and calculate what the actual distance is.

Some examples of map scales are...

- **1cm = 1km** - every 1cm you measure on the map represents 1km on the ground.

- **1:50 000** - every 1cm you measure on the map represents 50 000cm (or 500m) on the ground. Or, if you measure in inches, every inch you measure on the map represents 50 000 inches (about 1380 yards) on the ground.

Examples

Fitztown

Grange

Berniford

Hollow Trees

Scale 1cm = 5km

1 How far is it from Fitztown to Berniford?

On the map it is **7cm**, so **7 x 5 = 35km**.

2 I travel from Grange to Hollow Trees via Berniford. How much longer is this route than travelling directly from Grange to Hollow Trees?

| Grange to Berniford is **4cm** Berniford to Hollow Trees is **2.5cm** | **4 + 2.5 = 6.5cm** **6.5 x 5 = 32.5km** |
| Directly from Grange to Hollow Trees is **4.8cm** | **4.8cm x 5 = 24km** |

So it is **32.5 – 24 = 8.5km longer**.

? Now try these...

1 Use the diagram from the example above, but with a scale of 1cm = 10km, to work out the following:

  a) What is the distance from Fitztown to Hollow Trees by the shortest route?

  b) What is the difference between the distances from Grange to Fitztown and Grange to Berniford?

  c) What is the total length of all the roads on the map?

2 From Metropolis to Townsville, the angle from north is 210° clockwise. Townsville is 900km from Metropolis. Show this information on a scale drawing. Use the scale 1cm = 300km.

Location

You need to know...

- **how to use bearings to specify direction.**

When travelling, we rely on signposts and landmarks to find our way. However, in the air or at sea there is little to inform you of your location so navigators use bearings to find their way.

Bearings are a type of angle. However, they are always measured from north in a clockwise direction and are always given as 3 digits.

Remember the rules for angles on parallel lines? They can also be used when calculating bearings.

Examples

1 What bearing is Andrew travelling on?

Andrew is travelling on a bearing of 059°.

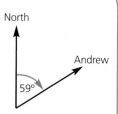

2 What bearing is Charlie travelling on?

> Small angles are easier to measure so the bearing can be calculated as
> **360° − 70° = 290°**

Charlie is travelling on a bearing of 290°.

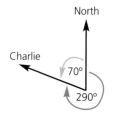

3 Give the bearing of B from A, and A from B.

> **180° − 115° = 65°**
> (co-interior angles)
> **360° − 65° = 295°**

The bearing of B from A is 115°. The bearing of A from B is 295°.

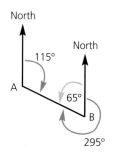

4 Give the bearing of D from C, and C from D.

The bearing of D from C is 105°. The bearing of C from D is 285°.

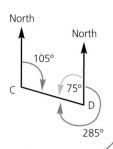

Now try these...

For the following diagrams, give the bearing of:

a) Y from X

b) X from Y

1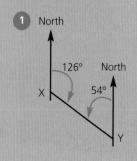

2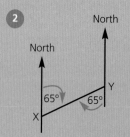

3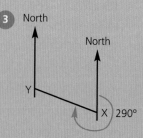

2-D Shapes

You need to know...

- **about the properties of quadrilaterals.**

A quadrilateral is a 4-sided, two-dimensional (2-D) shape, which has interior angles that add up to 360°.

Square	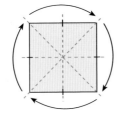	• Four equal sides. • Four lines of symmetry. • Rotational symmetry of order 4.
Rectangle	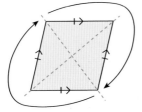	• Two pairs of equal sides. • Two lines of symmetry. • Rotational symmetry of order 2.
Rhombus	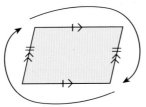	• Four equal sides. • Two pairs of parallel sides. • Two lines of symmetry. • Rotational symmetry of order 2.
Parallelogram	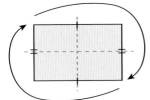	• Two pairs of equal sides and two pairs of parallel sides. • No lines of symmetry. • Rotational symmetry of order 2.
Trapezium	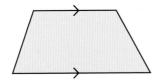	• No equal sides and one pair of parallel sides. • No line of symmetry. • No rotational symmetry ... unless it is an isosceles trapezium. 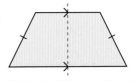
Kite	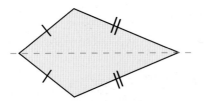	• Two pairs of equal sides. • One line of symmetry. • No rotational symmetry.

ℹ️ You need to know...

- **about the properties of different triangles.**

A triangle is a shape that has three sides.

Scalene Triangles		<ul><li>No equal sides and no equal angles.</li><li>No lines of symmetry.</li><li>No rotational symmetry.</li></ul>
Isosceles Triangles	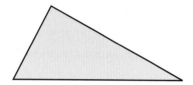	<ul><li>Two equal sides and two equal angles.</li><li>One line of symmetry.</li><li>No rotational symmetry.</li></ul>
Equilateral Triangles	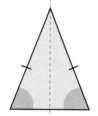	<ul><li>Three equal sides and three equal angles (60°).</li><li>Three lines of symmetry.</li><li>Rotational symmetry of order 3.</li></ul>
Right-angled Triangles	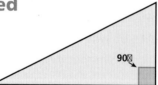	<ul><li>No equal sides and no equal angles.</li><li>No lines of symmetry.</li><li>No rotational symmetry ... unless it is also an isosceles triangle. 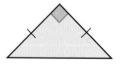</li></ul>

❓ Now try these...

1 Draw the following triangles and where applicable, indicate the lines of symmetry.

a) An equilateral triangle of side 4cm.

b) A right-angled isosceles triangle with the equal sides of length 5cm.

2 What type of triangle are the following statements describing?

a) I have two equal sides, two equal angles and one line of symmetry.

b) I have no equal angles, no equal sides, no lines of symmetry and none of my angles are 90°.

c) I have three equal sides and three equal angles.

You need to know...

- **about the properties of regular polygons.**

A **polygon** is a 2-D shape with many sides. Regular polygons have all their sides equal and all their angles equal.

Here are the names and properties of the first few regular polygons. A regular triangle is an **equilateral triangle** (see facing page.) A regular quadrilateral is a **square** (see p.75).

Regular Pentagon	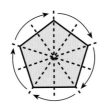	• Five equal sides and five equal angles. • Five lines of symmetry. • Rotational symmetry of order 5.
Regular Hexagon	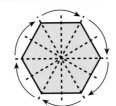	• Six equal sides and six equal angles. • Six lines of symmetry. • Rotational symmetry of order 6.
Regular Heptagon	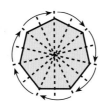	• Seven equal sides and seven equal angles. • Seven lines of symmetry. • Rotational symmetry of order 7.
Regular Octagon	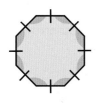 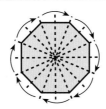	• Eight equal sides and eight equal angles. • Eight lines of symmetry. • Rotational symmetry of order 8.
Regular Nonagon	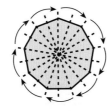	• Nine equal sides and nine equal angles. • Nine lines of symmetry. • Rotational symmetry of order 9.
Regular Decagon	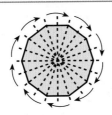	• Ten equal sides and ten equal angles. • Ten lines of symmetry. • Rotational symmetry of order 10.

i You need to know...

- **how to find the perimeters of simple shapes**
- **how to find the areas of shapes by counting squares.**

The **perimeter** of a 2-D shape is the total distance around the outside of the shape. Perimeter is usually measured in millimetres (mm), centimetres (cm), metres (m) or kilometres (km).

The perimeter of a shape can be found by counting along its edges using a grid of squares (of known side length) or by adding together the lengths of all its edges.

The **area** of a 2-D shape is a measure of how much space it covers. Area is measured in square units such as square millimetres (mm²), square centimetres (cm²), square meters (m²) and square kilometres (km²).

Area can be found by counting the total number of squares a shape covers on a grid.

To estimate the area of an irregular shape, count the squares that are more than half covered.

Examples

① Find the perimeters of these 2-D shapes. (Not drawn to scale).

a)
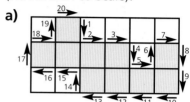
Perimeter = 20cm

b)
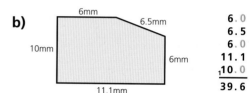
Perimeter = 39.6cm

② Find the areas of these 2-D shapes.

a)
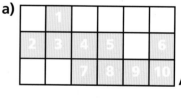
Area = 10cm²

b)

Area = 8cm²

? Now try these...

① Find the perimeter of these 2-D shapes.

a)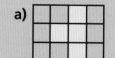

b)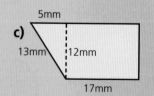

c)

② Find the area of these 2-D shapes. Remember you may have to estimate!

a)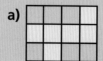

b)

c)

d)

③ Find both the area and perimeter of these 2-D shapes.

a)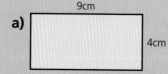

b)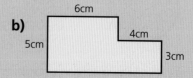

Perimeter and Area

i You need to know...

- **the formula for finding the area of a rectangle and how to use it.**

The standard formula for finding the area of a rectangle is:

Area = length x width or **A = ℓ x w**

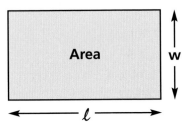

To calculate the area of this rectangle:

Area = ℓ x w
Area = 5cm x 3cm
Area = 15cm²

To prove the formula works, count the number of 1cm² squares that fit into the rectangle. You will see there are **3 rows of 5 squares**, which is **15** in total. Remember, in maths 'of' means 'multiply'. This is where the formula comes from.

Examples

① What is the area of this rectangle?

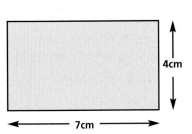

Area = ℓ x w
Area = 7 x 4
Area = 28cm²

② What is the area of this triangle?

> The area of a triangle is half the area of a rectangle

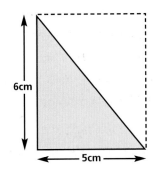

Area of rectangle = ℓ x w
so **Area of triangle = $\dfrac{\ell \text{ x w}}{2}$**

Area = $\dfrac{6 \text{ x } 5}{2}$

Area = $\dfrac{30}{2}$

Area = 15cm²

? Now try these...

Find the area of each shape.

1

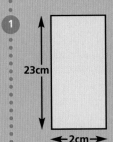

2

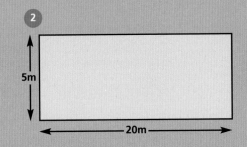

3

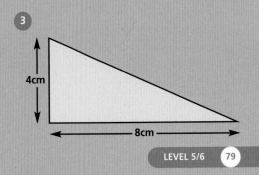

ℹ You need to know...

- **how to use the formulae for finding the area and circumference of a circle.**

It's important to know the names of the different parts of a circle.

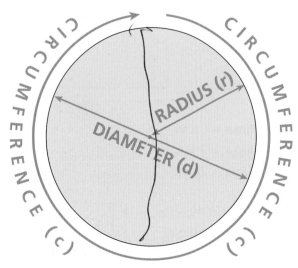

The circumference can be found using the formula:

> **Circumference = 2πr or πd**

The area of a circle is given by the formula:

> **Area = πr²**

π (pi) is simply a number: 3.141592653…. If you are not told the value for π in the question use the π button on your calculator, or 3.14.

Examples

Find the area and circumference of these circles.

1

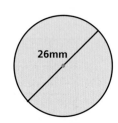

Area = π x r²
     = π x 4²
     = 3.14 x 16
     = 50.24cm²

Circumference = 2 x π x r
              = 2 x π x 4
              = 2 x 3.14 x 4
              = 25.12cm

2

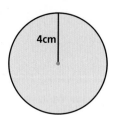

$r = \frac{d}{2}$

Area = π x r²
     = π x 13²
     = 3.14 x 169
     = 530.66mm²

Circumference = π x d
              = π x 26
              = 81.64mm

❓ Now try these...

1 Find the area and circumference of these circles. Watch the units!

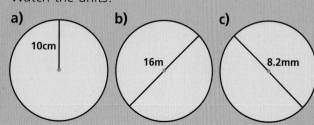

a) 10cm

b) 16m

c) 8.2mm

2 Find the area and total perimeter of this semicircle.

(Hint – find the area and circumference of the full circle then divide by two. Don't forget to add on the straight edge to get the perimeter.)

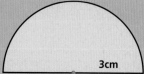

3cm

Perimeter and Area

ℹ You need to know...

- **how to find an unknown side length in a shape using its area measurement.**

For shapes like rectangles and circles, where there is a standard formula for finding the area, it is also possible to work backwards and use the area to find an unknown length measurement, e.g. the width/length of a rectangle or the radius of a circle.

Examples

Calculate the missing lengths in these shapes.

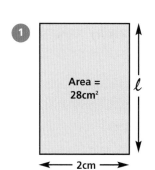

① Area = 28cm², 2cm wide, length ℓ

$$\ell \times w = \text{Area}$$
$$\ell \times 2 = 28$$
$$\frac{\ell \times 2}{2} = \frac{28}{2}$$
$$\ell = 14\text{cm}$$

> This is just like solving a linear equation in algebra (see p.47)

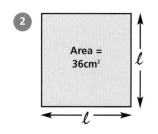

② Area = 36cm², side ℓ

$$\ell \times \ell = \text{Area}$$
$$\ell^2 = 36$$
$$\sqrt{\ell^2} = \sqrt{36}$$
$$\ell = 6\text{cm}$$

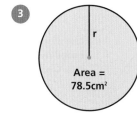

③ Area = 78.5cm², radius r

$$\pi \times r^2 = \text{Area}$$
$$3.14 \times r^2 = 78.5$$
$$\frac{3.14 \times r^2}{3.14} = \frac{78.5}{3.14}$$
$$r^2 = 25$$
$$r = \sqrt{25}$$
$$r = 5\text{cm}$$

❓ Now try these...

Find the missing lengths in these shapes.

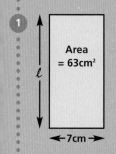

① Area = 63cm², ℓ, 7cm

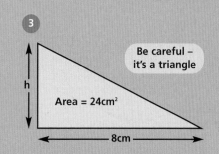

② Area = 300m², w, 20m

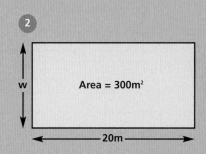

③ Area = 24cm², h, 8cm. Be careful – it's a triangle

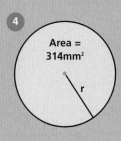

④ Area = 314mm², r

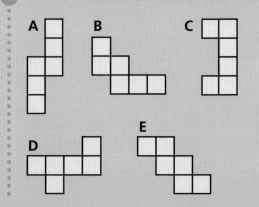

ⓘ You need to know...

- **the words used to describe the features of 3-D solids**
- **how to make 3-D models by linking edges and faces.**

To make a model of a 3-D shape, you start with a **net**. A net is a 2-D plan or pattern that is cut and folded to make the 3-D shape.

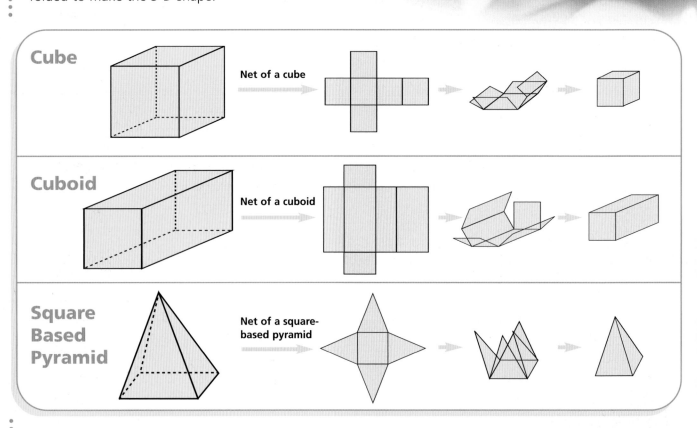

Cube — Net of a cube

Cuboid — Net of a cuboid

Square Based Pyramid — Net of a square-based pyramid

It's also important to know the words used to describe 3-D solids.

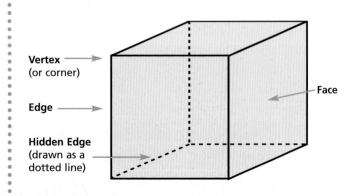

Vertex (or corner)

Edge

Hidden Edge (drawn as a dotted line)

Face

❓ Now try these...

1. Which of these nets would make a cube?

A B C

D E

i You need to know...

- **how to use common 2-D representations of 3-D solids.**

Isometric paper can be used to draw 3-D solids. Isometric paper consists of dots or a grid arranged in equilateral triangles.

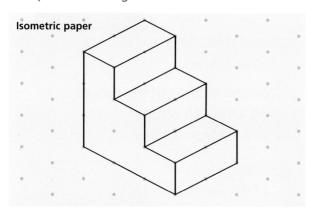

Isometric paper

Plans and elevations show what a 3-D solid looks like from different viewpoints.

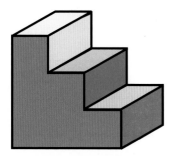

A plan shows what the solid looks like from above. Elevations show what it looks like from the front and the side.

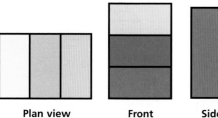

Plan view   **Front elevation**   **Side elevation**

A cross-section drawing shows what a 3-D solid would look like if you sliced through it.

A **prism** is a 3-D solid with a uniform cross-section. That means its cross-section is exactly the same all the way through.

Cylinder

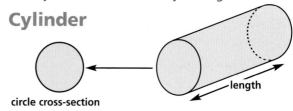

circle cross-section   length

Triangular prism

triangle cross-section

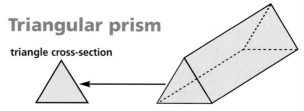

(You can also have pentagonal, hexagonal, octagonal, etc. prisms)

Cone

A cone is not a prism because it gets smaller towards the top.

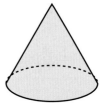

Sphere

A sphere is definitely not a prism!

? Now try these...

1. Draw the plan view, front elevation and side elevation of this solid.

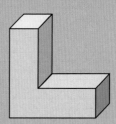

2. Draw the net of a cylinder.

Examples

1. Find the volume of this cuboid.

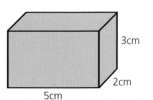

If the cuboid was made of 1cm³ cubes it would look like this:

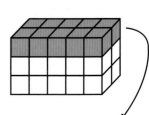

The top layer is made from 10 cubes and there are 2 more identical layers below ...

So the volume of the cuboid is

10 + 10 + 10 = 30cm³

or 3 x 10cm³ = 30cm³

i You need to know...

- **how to find the volume of cuboids by counting cubes.**

The volume of a 3-D solid is a measure of how much space it takes up. Volume is measured in cubic units such as mm³, cm³, m³, and even km³ for really big objects!

The volume of a 3-D solid can be found by counting the number of 1cm³ cubes that fit into it. This is a 1cm³ cube:

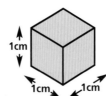

If the length measurements are given in m³, you would use 1m³ cubes instead, and so on.

2. Find the volume of this 4cm cube.

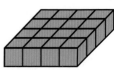

Again, imagine the cube is made from 1cm³ cubes:

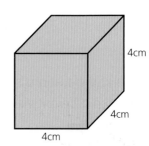

The top layer is made from 16 cubes and there are 3 more identical layers below ...

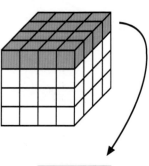

So the volume of the cube is

16 + 16 + 16 + 16 = 64cm³

or 4 x 16cm³ = 64cm³

? Now try these...

Calculate the volume of each cuboid.

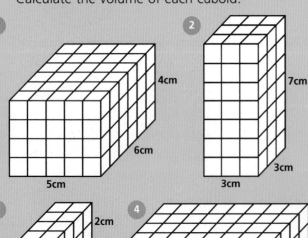

Volume

ℹ You need to know...

- **the formula for finding the volume of a cuboid and how to use it.**

The formula for the volume of a cuboid is
Volume = length x width x height
or **V = ℓ x w x h**.

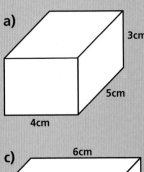

The formula for the volume of a cube is
V = ℓ x ℓ x ℓ or V = ℓ³.

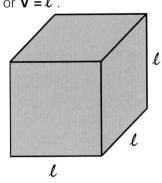

Examples

1 Find the volume of this cuboid.

V = ℓ x w x h
V = 7 x 3 x 3
V = 63cm³

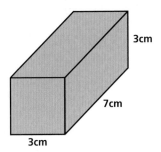

3cm
7cm
3cm

2 Find the volume of this cube.

V = ℓ³
V = 4.5³
(or **4.5 x 4.5 x 4.5**)
V = 91.125cm³

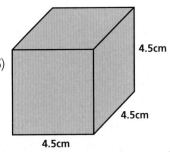

4.5cm
4.5cm
4.5cm

？ Now try these...

1 Find the volume of each of these cubes and cuboids.

a)
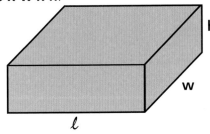
3cm
5cm
4cm

b)
5cm
5cm
5cm

c)
6cm
2cm
3cm

2 What is the volume of a box measuring 15cm by 5cm by 10cm?

3 How many 1cm³ cubes could you fit inside a box 6cm long, 4cm wide and 3cm high?

You need to know...

- **how to recognise reflective symmetry in 2-D shapes.**

A 2-D shape has reflective or line symmetry if one side is a perfect mirror image of the other. The line of symmetry (or mirror line) is usually shown using a dotted line. Shapes can have more than one line of symmetry.

Line of symmetry

Examples

1. Use dotted lines to draw the lines of symmetry on the letters below.

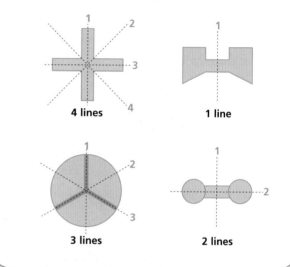

2. Use dotted lines to draw the lines of symmetry on the shapes below.

4 lines

1 line

3 lines

2 lines

? Now try these...

1. Are there any other capital letters that have line symmetry. If so, draw them and mark on their lines of symmetry.

2. Draw the lines of symmetry (if there are any) on these road signs.

3. Draw the reflections of these shapes on the other side of the mirror line.

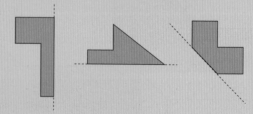

Diagonal mirror lines are tricky. This may help you.

Symmetry

You need to know...

- **how to recognise and visualise plane symmetry in 3-D shapes.**

3-D solids have plane symmetry if they can be cut into two identical pieces that are mirror images of each other. The line of the cut through the shape is called the plane of symmetry. The examples below show one plane of symmetry for each shape but there are more.

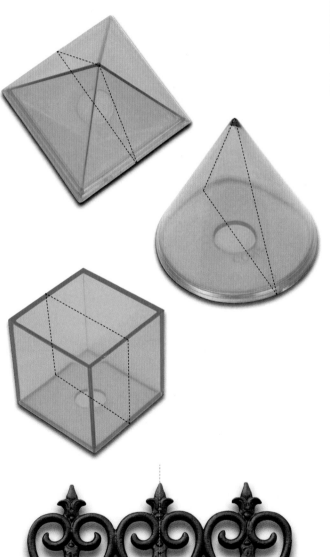

Example

1. How many planes of symmetry does this prism have? Draw them in.

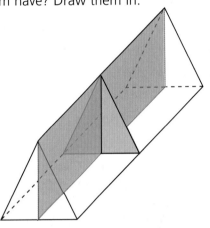

It has 2 planes of symmetry.

? Now try these...

1. A cube has lots of planes of symmetry. One is shown on this page. Can you draw another?

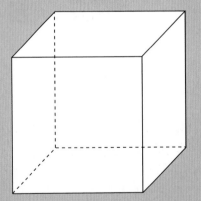

2. A cylinder has lots of planes of symmetry. Draw two.

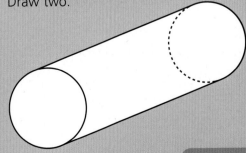

You need to know...

- **how to recognise and visualise rotational symmetry in 2-D shapes.**

A 2-D shape has rotational symmetry if you can rotate the shape into different positions and it looks the same as it did to start with. If the shape has two of these positions we say it has rotational symmetry of order 2.

These letters have rotational symmetry.

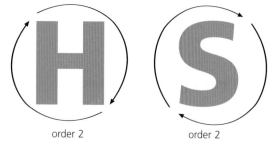

order 2   order 2

These shapes have rotational symmetry...   ... but these do not.

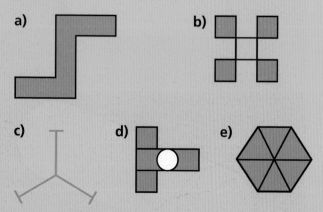

order 3   order 4

? Now try these...

1. State the order of rotational symmetry of these shapes.

a)
b)

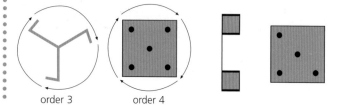

c)   d)   e)

Examples

1. What order of rotational symmetry do these letters have?

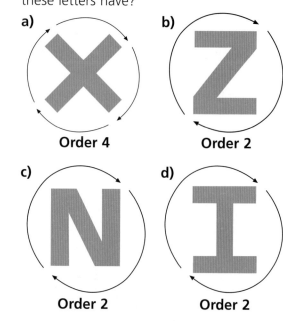

a)   b)

Order 4   Order 2

c)   d)

Order 2   Order 2

2. What is the order of rotational symmetry of this shape?

If you find it difficult to visualise rotational symmetry, trace or copy the shape and turn the paper to see if it looks the same in any other positions.

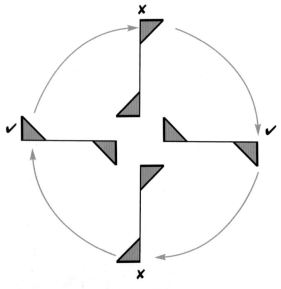

Order of rotational symmetry = 2.

ⓘ You need to know...

- **how to recognise if a shape tessellates.**

If lots of examples of the same shape can be fitted together exactly, with no gaps, we say it tessellates. These shapes tessellate…

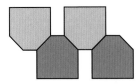
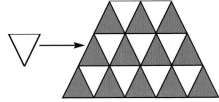
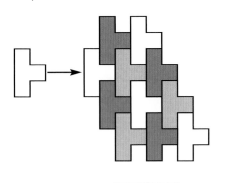

…but these won't…

Examples

① Will this shape produce a tessellation?

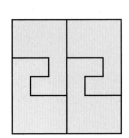
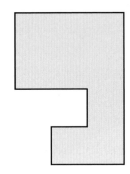

Yes.

② Does this shape tessellate?

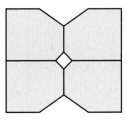
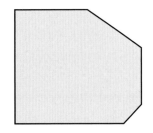

No. It leaves gaps.

❓ Now try these...

Try to produce a tessellation with each shape below and state whether it will or will not tessellate. Remember the shapes may fit together in more than one way.

a)   b)   c)   d)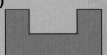

e)   f)   g)   h)

i You need to know...

- **how to reflect a 2-D shape in a mirror line.**

In a reflection, everything that appears on one side of the mirror line must appear on the other side too. The size and the shape of the object being reflected remain exactly the same, but its position is reversed to produce a mirror image. A reflected image is always congruent to the original shape (see p.96). This topic is closely linked to line symmetry (see p.86).

1 Mark two points (● and ●) on the mirror line.

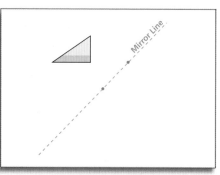

2 Lay a sheet of tracing paper over the shape and mirror line. Trace the shape, the mirror line and the two points.

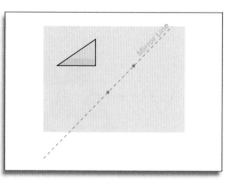

3 Flip the tracing paper over making sure you line up the mirror line and the two points. This shows you the position of the reflected image.

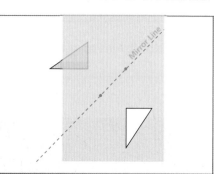

4 Draw the image and label it.

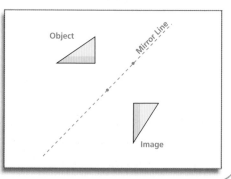

Examples

Reflect these shapes in their mirror lines.

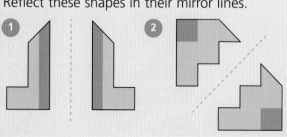

? Now try these...

Copy these shapes and reflect them in their mirror lines.

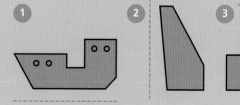

Reflections

ℹ You need to know...

- **how to identify and describe the mirror line of a reflected object.**

Here are some common lines that you should know, A line with the equation **x = 'a number'** is a vertical line through that number on the x-axis.

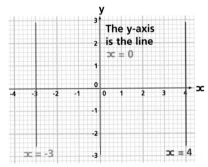

A line with the equation **y = 'a number'** is a horizontal line through that number on the y-axis.

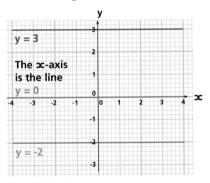

The line **y = x** is the diagonal line where the numbers in the coordinates are the same, i.e. it goes through (-1,-1), (2,2), (5,5), etc.

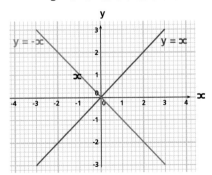

The other diagonal is **y = -x** (see p.58). In this case, although the numerical values of the x and y coordinates are the same, one will have a minus sign (except for when it goes through (0,0)!), i.e. it goes through (-3,3), (-4,4), (2,-2) etc.

Examples

1 Reflect the shape in the line y = 0. Label the image A.

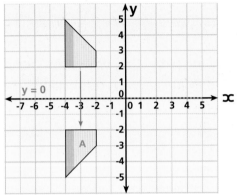

2 Reflect the shape in the line y = x. Label the image B.

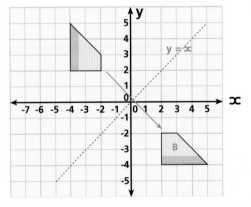

❓ Now try these...

1 Reflect the shape in the following lines of reflection:

a) y = 1. Label the image A.

b) y = -x. Label the image B.

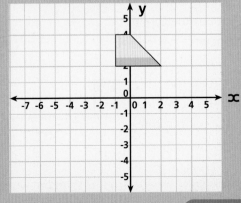

You need to know...

- **how to rotate 2-D shapes about a point.**

Rotation is simply the act of rotating an object about a fixed point, which is called the centre of rotation. The size and shape of the object remain exactly the same. Only its position changes. A rotated image is always congruent to the original shape (see p.96). This topic is closely linked to rotational symmetry (see p.88).

To describe a rotation, you need to give the angle, direction and centre of rotation. The angle can be given as a fraction of a turn (such as a quarter turn) or in degrees (such as 90°). The direction can be clockwise or anti-clockwise.

1 Draw a dotted line from the centre of rotation to the nearest point on the shape. Place the baseline of your protractor on the dotted line so the cross is over the centre of rotation.

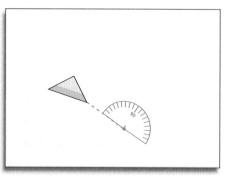

2 Draw the angle of rotation using another dotted line. Then place tracing paper on top and draw the shape on it.

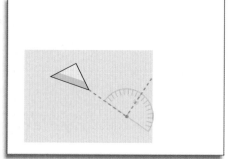

3 Place your pen or a compass on the centre of rotation and rotate your tracing paper (90° clockwise in this example).

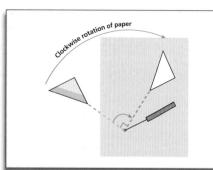

4 Using the tracing paper as a guide, mark each corner, and then draw in the edges. This new shape is called an **image**.

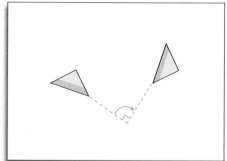

Examples

① Rotate this shape 90° anti-clockwise about the centre shown.

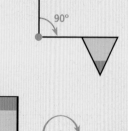

② Rotate this shape a half turn about the centre shown.

Now try these...

Copy and rotate the following shapes as instructed.

① A quarter turn anti-clockwise around the centre shown.

② 180° around the centre shown.

③ 90° clockwise around the centre shown.

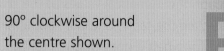

Rotations

ⓘ You need to know...

- **how to rotate objects about a given centre of rotation.**

Rotations can also be done on graph paper using axes. Again, you need to specify the angle and direction of the rotation, but this time the centre of rotation is given by coordinates. You can still use tracing paper, as before.

① To rotate triangle A 90° clockwise about the centre (-1,1), carefully trace the axes and shape on the tracing paper.

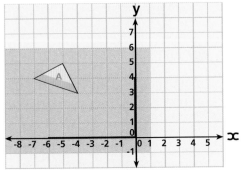

② Place the point of your compass on the centre of rotation (-1,1) and rotate the paper clockwise.

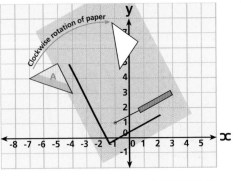

③ After 90° rotation, use the tracing paper as a guide and mark each corner of the shape on the graph paper.

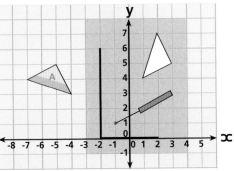

④ Remove the tracing paper and draw in the edges to complete the image.

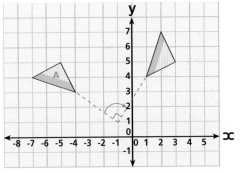

Example

Rotate the triangle ...

a) 90° clockwise about (0,0). Label it A.

b) 180° about (-1,1). Label it B.

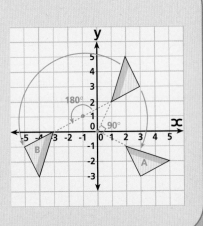

? Now try these...

① Rotate triangle A ...

a) 90° anti-clockwise around (0,0). Label it B.

b) 180° around (0,-3). Label it C.

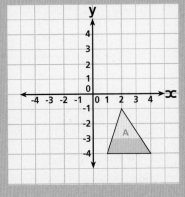

You need to know...

- **how to describe and perform a translation using a distance and a direction.**

A translation is where you 'slide' an object into a new position. The size and shape of the object remain exactly the same, so the translated image is always congruent to the original shape. To describe a translation you must specify the direction and the distance the shape is being moved. However, instead of saying 'two to the right and three up', you use a vector.

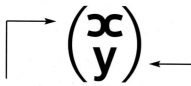

the **x** number tells us how many units to move horizontally. Movement to the right (→) is positive, left (←) is negative.

the **y** number tells us how many units to move vertically. Movement up (↑) is positive, down (↓) is negative.

Examples

1. Translate shape A by vector $\begin{pmatrix} 4 \\ 0 \end{pmatrix}$ (4 squares to the right).

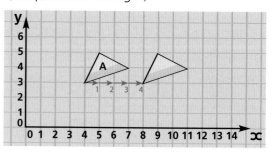

2. Translate shape B by vector $\begin{pmatrix} -1 \\ -2 \end{pmatrix}$ (1 square to the left and 2 squares down).

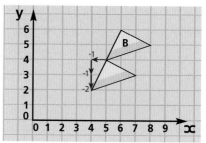

Now try these...

1

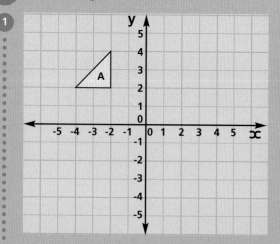

a) Translate triangle A by vector $\begin{pmatrix} 5 \\ 1 \end{pmatrix}$. Label it B.

b) Translate triangle A by vector $\begin{pmatrix} 0 \\ -3 \end{pmatrix}$. Label it C.

c) Describe the translation from B to C.

2

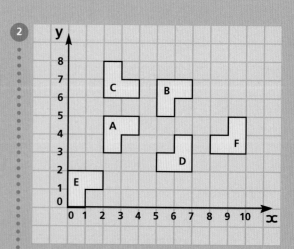

Which of these are translations?

a) A to B   b) C to D   c) A to E

d) B to D   e) E to B   f) D to F

Give the vector for those which are.

Transformations

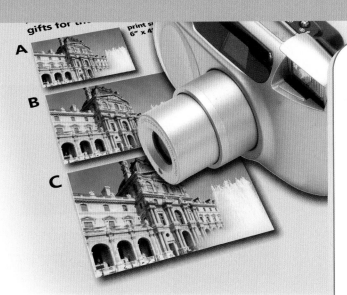

You need to know...

- **how to visualise and recognise enlargements of shapes**
- **how to produce enlargements specified by a centre of enlargement and a positive scale factor.**

An **enlargement** changes the size of a shape, but the ratio of the sides stays the same. To describe an enlargement you need to give the centre of enlargement and the scale factor. The length of each of the shape's sides is multiplied by the scale factor to give the side lengths for the enlarged image.

Examples

1 Enlarge shape A by scale factor 2. The centre of enlargement is (0,0).

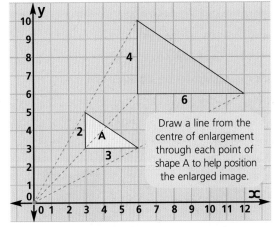

Draw a line from the centre of enlargement through each point of shape A to help position the enlarged image.

2 Enlarge shape A by scale factor 3. The centre of enlargement is (3,1).

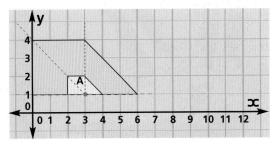

Now try these...

1

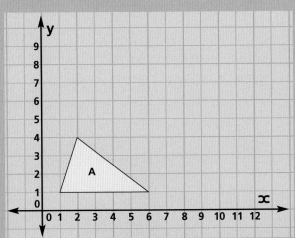

Enlarge triangle A by scale factor 2 using the origin (0,0) as the centre of enlargement. Label your image B.

2

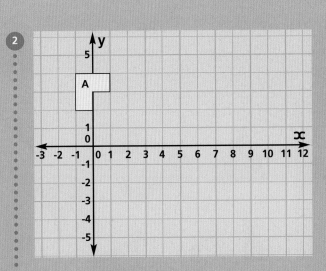

Enlarge shape A by scale factor 3 using (-3,5) as the centre of enlargement. Label your image B.

ⓘ You need to know...

- **how to recognise congruent shapes.**

When a shape is translated, rotated or reflected the lengths and angles of the image are the same as the lengths and angles of the original. If two (or more) shapes are exactly the same shape and size they are said to be **congruent**.

These four boys are congruent.

Examples

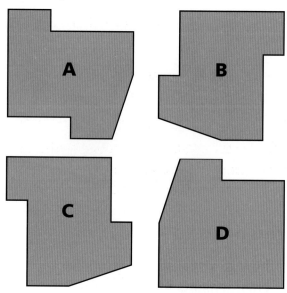

1 Is shape B congruent to A?

Shape B is a rotation of shape A. The two shapes are congruent.

2 Is shape C congruent to A?

Shape C is a reflection and rotation of shape. The two shapes are congruent.

3 Is shape D congruent to A?

Shape D is not congruent to shape A.

❓ Now try these...

1 Which triangles are congruent?

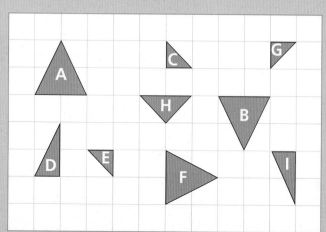

2 Draw 2 shapes that are congruent to this shape. Try to make them look different by reflecting them or rotating them but make sure they're congruent.

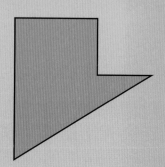

Congruent & Similar Shapes

You need to know...

- **how to recognise similar shapes.**

Shapes are similar if they are exactly the same shape, but one is an enlargement of the other. The angles are the same but the side lengths are all increased by the same scale factor (see p.95).

Any two circles are mathematically similar, as are any two squares because all four sides are always equal and each interior angle will always be 90°. Two rectangles are not necessarily similar because the ratio of their side lengths (width to length) can vary.

Example

Which of these shapes are similar to A?

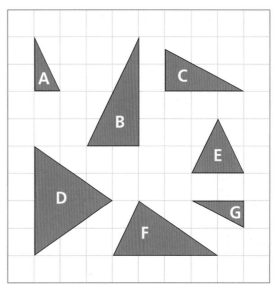

Shape B is similar to A. It is enlarged by a scale factor of 2 and reflected. Shape C is similar to A. It is enlarged by a scale factor of 1.5, rotated and reflected. Shape G is congruent to A. It is rotated and reflected.

? **Now try these...**

1 Which of these shapes are similar?

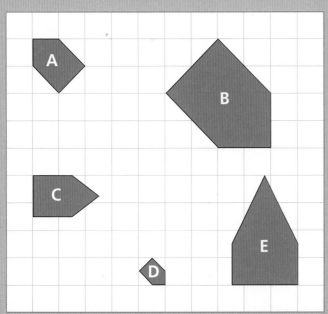

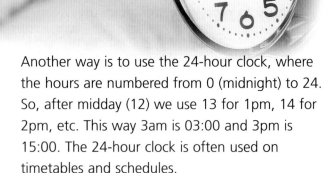

ⓘ You need to know...

- **how to use standard units of time.**

Here are the standard units used for measuring time. You will already be familiar with them, but make sure you learn all the equivalent values too.

60 seconds = 1 minute
60 minutes = 1 hour
24 hours = 1 day
7 days = 1 week
365 days = ⎫
52 weeks = ⎬ **1 year**
366 days = 1 leap year (extra day is 29th February)
10 years = 1 decade
100 years = 1 century
1000 years = 1 millennium

Time can be measured using 12-hour and 24-hour clocks. We tend to use the 12-hour clock when talking about time in our day-to-day lives.

This is a 12-hour clock. It shows 7 o'clock, but you don't know if it's in the morning or in the evening. We use 7am to mean before midday and 7pm to mean after midday to be sure.

Another way is to use the 24-hour clock, where the hours are numbered from 0 (midnight) to 24. So, after midday (12) we use 13 for 1pm, 14 for 2pm, etc. This way 3am is 03:00 and 3pm is 15:00. The 24-hour clock is often used on timetables and schedules.

Examples

① A CD has a playing time of 120 minutes. What is that in hours?

1 hour = 60 minutes
120 ÷ 60 minutes = 2 hours

② My digital watch says it is 20:20. What time is this using a 12-hour clock? (Don't forget am or pm!)

20 – 12 = 8. Because 20 is bigger than 12, we know that it is a pm time, and subtracting 12 gives the correct hour. The minutes remain the same.
So it is 8.20pm.

❓ Now try these...

① Daniel starts a new job for which the annual (i.e. yearly) salary is £10 400. He is paid weekly. How much will he receive each week?

② Alex is looking for a new job. She has seen two jobs advertised. Job A is offering £825 a month and Job B is offering £5.50 an hour.
   a) If she works 35 hours a week in each job, calculate how much she would earn from each job in a year.
   b) Which job has the higher salary?

③ Complete this table showing 12-hour and 24-hour clock times.

12-hour	8.30am	9.45pm			12.00am	
24-hour			13.05	22.40		12.00

④ Use the rhyme '30 days has September, April, June and November. All the rest have 31, except for February alone which has 28 days clear and 29 in each leap year' to help you work out how many days...
   a) from 18 May to 13 June
   b) from 17 August to 23 October (Don't forget September!)

Time

You need to know...

- **how to perform calculations involving time**
- **how to perform time calculations in which fractions of an hour need to be treated as fractions or decimals.**

We often measure time in fractions of an hour i.e. $\frac{1}{4}$ of an hour, $\frac{1}{2}$ an hour, $\frac{3}{4}$ of an hour. Remember, the whole is 1 hour (or 60 minutes) so...

$\frac{1}{4}$ **of an hour =**

$\frac{1}{4} \times 60 = 15$ minutes $\longrightarrow \frac{15}{60} = 0.25$ hours

$\frac{1}{2}$ **an hour =**

$\frac{1}{2} \times 60 = 30$ minutes $\longrightarrow \frac{30}{60} = 0.5$ hours

$\frac{3}{4}$ **of an hour =**

$\frac{3}{4} \times 60 = 45$ minutes $\longrightarrow \frac{45}{60} = 0.75$ hours

Make sure you don't mistake times for decimals. For example, 7.20 represents 7 hours and 20 minutes *not* 7.2 hours (which would be 7 hours and 12 minutes)!

Examples

Crogglethwaite	0720	0840	1022	1245
Daisy Vale	0735	0855	1039	1300
Barrowby Wood	0747	-	1055	1312
Hathersedge	0752	0909	1103	1317

Look at this timetable. It shows 4 trains from Crogglethwaite to Hathersedge which pass through Daisy Vale and Barrowby Wood on the way. Notice one of the trains doesn't stop at Barrowby Wood.

1 How long does it take the first train to get from Crogglethwaite to Hathersedge?

It takes 07:52 – 07:20 = **32 minutes** (remember to subtract the minutes first, then do the hours)

2 I want to leave Daisy Vale and be in Hathersedge before midday. What is the last train I can catch and how long will the journey take?

The last train arrives in Hathersedge too late so I'll have to get the **10:39 from Daisy Vale**. It arrives in Hathersedge at 11:03. The journey takes **24 minutes**. (From 10:39 there are 21 minutes until 11:00 then add on the extra 3 minutes after 11:00.)

Now try these...

1 a) Use the timetable above to work out all the journey times from Crogglethwaite to Hathersedge.

b) One train is much slower than the others. Which one is it?

2 Use the timetable above to answer this question. I have to get from Daisy Vale to Barrowby Wood and arrive before 11am. Which train should I catch, and how long will the journey take?

3 Caroline needs to go shopping. It takes 25 minutes to drive to the shops and 25 minutes to drive home again. It will take her $\frac{3}{4}$ of an hour to shop. How long will the entire trip take? Give your answer in hours to 2 d.p.

4 A coach leaves at 11.35am. The journey takes 2 hours and 50 minutes. At what time does it arrive at its destination? (Give your answer in 24-hour time).

You need to know...

- **how to collect data using observation**
- **how to gather data from secondary sources.**

Information that is collected for a specific purpose, e.g. to help answer a question, investigate an idea or prove a theory, is called **data**.

If you collect the data yourself it is called **primary data**. One of the easiest ways of collecting primary data is through **observation**. For example, you could count the number of buses that stop at a particular bus stop in a one-hour period.

Data that can be counted in whole numbers like this is called **discrete data**.

When you collect data you need to keep a record in a frequency table or tally chart (see p.102-103).

Secondary data is data that has been collected by somebody else. You can find examples everywhere e.g. in books or on the internet.

Secondary data can be presented in lots of different ways, including tables, charts, spreadsheets and databases. When using secondary sources like these, it is important to make sure that the information is relevant - it must help you complete your task, otherwise it is useless!

? Now try these...

1 Look at the table in Example 1.
   a) Your mum is going to London for the weekend and would like to see St James's Park. Which tour(s) would you recommend?
   b) She would also like to visit Westminster Abbey. Is there a tour that includes Westminster Abbey and St James's Park?
   c) If you were visiting London on Saturday, what is the cheapest tour available?

Example

A London tourist office publishes a list of guided tours available each week. Here is their list for the week beginning 12th September.

Tour	Days	Price
Famous Landmarks Tower of London, Tower Bridge, St Paul's, Buckingham Palace, Big Ben, Westminster Abbey	Tuesday, Thursday, Saturday, Sunday	£45.00 p.p.
Parks and Gardens Regent's Park, London Zoo, Hyde Park, Kensington Gardens, St James's Park, Green Park	Wednesday, Friday, Sunday	£25.50 p.p.
Star Attractions Tower Bridge, London Dungeons, London Eye, Westminster Abbey, Buckingham Palace	Monday, Wednesday, Friday	£60.00 p.p.
Royal London Tower of London, Buckingham Palace, St James's Park, Kensington Palace	Monday, Saturday, Sunday	£25.50 p.p.
Museums and Galleries Tate Modern, National Gallery, British Museum, Natural History Museum, V&A	Tuesday, Thursday, Saturday	£17.50 p.p.

a) Your friend will be in London on Wednesday, Thursday and Friday. She wants to visit Buckingham Palace. Which tour(s) would you recommend?

The Famous Landmarks, Star Attractions and Royal London tours all visit Buckingham Palace. However, only the Famous Landmarks and Star Attractions are available on the days she is there.

b) She doesn't want to spend more than £50. Which tour would you recommend?

Star Attractions is too expensive. Famous Landmarks is within budget at £45.00.

Collecting Data

ℹ You need to know...

- **how to collect continuous data.**

In addition to observation, data can be collected by carrying out a survey. For example, you could ask all the pupils in your class what their favourite colour is or how much pocket money they get each week.

Another method is to take measurements, e.g. height, weight, time, temperature. Data collected this way is called **continuous data**.

Continuous data can take any value in a certain range. For example, if you were measuring the height of people in your class, you would get all sorts of results, not just whole numbers (e.g. 162.5cm, 160cm, 173.8cm…).

When you collect continuous data you must be consistent. For example, use the same measuring equipment, the same units and the same level of accuracy for each measurement – if you round one number to 2 decimal places, make sure you do the same with all of them!

You are likely to get a wide range of different results when collecting continuous data. Depending on what you are looking for, you can record each measurement individually or you can record in a group called a **class interval** (see p.103).

Examples

1 Marcus thinks that the boys in his class play sport more often than the girls. He conducts a survey to find out how many times a week each pupil in his class plays sport. What type of data is this?

He is asking the pupils to **count** how many times they play sport in a week. They will give answers like once, twice, three times etc. This is **discrete data**.

2 Marcus wants to know if there is a link between the amount of sport pupils do and their body weight. He weighs all the pupils in his class. What type of data is this?

Weight is a **measurement**. This is an example of **continuous data**.

? Now try these...

1 For each of these examples, say whether it is an example of discrete or continuous data.
  a) Recording how many trains stop at a station in 1 day.
  b) Recording the length of time each train waits at a station.
  c) Recording the height of a sunflower over a period of time as it grows from a seed.
  d) Recording how many leaves each sunflower has when fully grown.

2 Look at question 1c). How would you ensure that the data collected was consistent? Give four ways.

You need to know...

- **how to organise discrete data by recording it in a frequency table.**

When data is collected it needs to be recorded in a way that makes it easy to use. One method of recording data is using a frequency table or tally chart. **Frequency** means 'how many', and a **frequency table** shows how many there are of each item.

Tally marks are recorded in sets of five 𝍤 so they can be counted easily. The total number of tally marks for each item is the frequency.

When you collect data that is spread over a large range of results it is more convenient to put the data into groups. These groups are called **class intervals**.

In a grouped frequency table there should be fewer than 10 class intervals and they should all be the same width. For example, if you were creating a frequency table for journey times you might use 1-10 minutes, 11-20 minutes, 21-30 minutes etc as the groups (notice that each group has a range of 10 minutes).

Examples

1 Draw a frequency table for the results of a survey of what 30 students had for breakfast: cereal, cereal, nothing, toast, toast, drink only, drink only, cereal, toast, nothing, cereal, drink only, cereal, cereal, drink only, cereal, drink only, cereal, nothing, nothing, toast, cereal, cereal, toast, cooked, drink only, cooked, toast, drink only, drink only

Breakfast	Tally	Frequency
Cereal	𝍤 𝍤	10
Toast	𝍤	6
Cooked	||	2
Drink only	𝍤 |||	8
Nothing	||||	4
	Total	30

Add all the frequencies to find the total – it should be the same as the number of students who took part in the survey

2 Draw a frequency table for the maths test results for a class of 30 students:
45, 35, 46, 58, 38, 46, 24, 56, 53, 31, 55, 45, 28, 44, 52, 55, 60, 46, 56, 26, 43, 54, 19, 47, 28, 49, 47, 45, 18, 33

Class interval	Tally	Frequency
1-10		0
11-20	||	2
21-30	||||	4
31-40	||||	4
41-50	𝍤 𝍤		11
51-60	𝍤 ||||	9
	Total	30

Now try these...

1 A class did a traffic survey for geography. They noted down the vehicles that drove past the school in a 5-minute period. Their results were:
car, car, lorry, car, car, bus, lorry, car, van, bus, lorry, car, car, car, car, van, van, lorry, car, car, lorry, lorry, car, car, car, van, car, lorry, car, bus
Draw and complete the tally chart.

2 28 children timed their journey to school to the nearest minute:
5, 7, 3, 9, 10, 2, 5, 14, 12, 6, 12, 8, 23, 9, 12, 5, 9, 5, 5, 19, 11, 12, 10, 3, 8, 10, 15, 8
a) Draw a frequency table with 5 classes of equal width and put this data in it.
b) How many pupils took 11-15 minutes to get to school?
c) Which journey time had the highest frequency?

Organising Data

You need to know...

- **how to design and use two-way tables**
- **how to record continuous data in a frequency table using appropriate class intervals.**

Two-way tables are a simple way to record two sets of related information. They allow you to examine the information, find out more and fill in missing information, which can be very useful.

Continuous data can be recorded in a **grouped frequency table** with suitable **class intervals**. Class intervals are groups of equal width with no overlap. They are either written as open intervals in the form 1-, 10-, etc. (look at the table in Example 1) or as inequalities in the form 1≤h<10, 10≤h<20, etc. The size of each class interval will depend on the range of the data. You should always have fewer than 10 groups.

Examples

1. The heights of a group of 25 children were recorded to the nearest centimetre:
135, 120, 140, 134, 128, 141, 149, 156, 139, 152, 142, 153, 152, 120, 127, 129, 147, 139, 154, 148, 155, 143, 137, 129, 152
Draw a tally chart to represent the data.

> The range of heights is **156 – 120 = 36cm**.
> Choose four class intervals of width 10cm.

Height (cm)	Tally	Frequency
120-	⦀⦀	6
130-	⦀	5
140-	⦀⦀	7
150-	⦀⦀	7
	Total	25

2. A survey of whether 240 Year 8 and Year 9 students used the school library during the lunch break or after school showed that 20 out of 100 Year 8 students used the library after school whilst a total of 160 students used the library at lunchtime. Create a two-way table, insert the data you have been given and fill in the missing information.

	Year 8	Year 9	Total
Lunchtime	80	80	160
After school	20	60	80
Total	100	140	240

Now try these...

1. The temperature (in °C), in different cities throughout the world was recorded on one day:
31, 9, 12, 24, 17, 6, 19, 11, 21, 33, 13, 17, 5, 36, 22, 7, 14, 25, 9, 18, 4, 21, 28, 2, 10, 27, 12, 17, 19, 17
Draw a frequency table for the data, using suitable class intervals.

2. Two local secondary schools have a total of 3125 students. North Park has 1875 students of which 968 are boys, whilst South Street has only 549 boys. Draw a two-way table, enter the data you have and calculate the missing numbers.

You need to know...

- **how to construct bar charts and pictograms.**

Discrete data can be displayed using a variety of graphs. These give you a 'picture' of the data.

Whichever graph you use to display your data, make sure you give it a title, label the axes and include a key so it is clear what it shows.

A **pictogram** uses symbols or pictures to represent data.

Favourite Sports

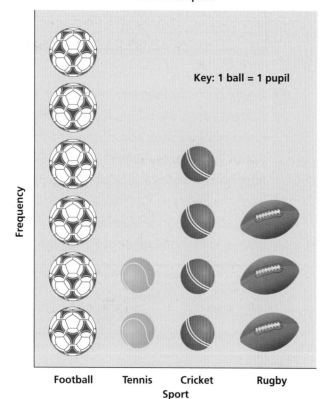

The diagram above shows pupils' favourite sports. Each symbol represents 1 pupil and 15 pupils were asked in total. If 150 pupils had been asked it would take a very long time to draw 150 symbols, so instead you can use one symbol to represent 10 pupils. If, for example, 75 pupils had chosen football as their favourite sport, you would draw 7 whole footballs and 1 half football to show this.

A **bar chart** uses bars to represent the data.

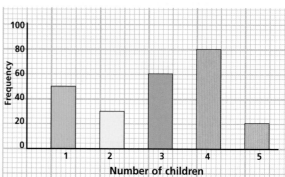

In a bar chart, there is a gap between each bar. The height of each bar shows the frequency. The bars are usually drawn vertically. However, they can also be drawn horizontally, in this case the frequency is shown by the length of the bar.

The tallest (or longest) bar in a bar chart shows which item or value has the highest frequency. This means it is the most popular. The shortest bar represents the item or value that occurs the least.

Vertical line graphs are similar to bar charts but lines replace the bars.

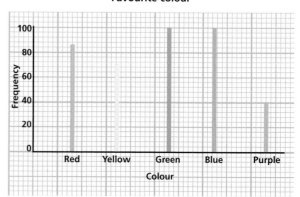

If you draw the lines in different colours make sure you include a key so it is clear what each colour represents. Alternatively, you can write underneath each line, like in a bar chart.

Displaying Data

Examples

A survey of the items sold in a school tuck shop produced the following results.

Item	Frequency
Sweets	55
Crisps	60
Biscuits	25
Fruit	30
Drinks	60

1 **a)** Draw a pictogram to represent this information.

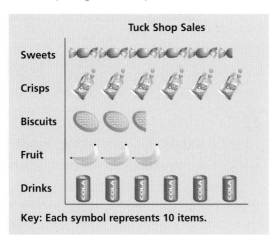

Tuck Shop Sales

Sweets
Crisps
Biscuits
Fruit
Drinks

Key: Each symbol represents 10 items.

b) Which item sold the least?
   Biscuits (25).
c) How many items were sold in total?
   55 + 60 + 25 + 30 + 60 = 230.

2 **a)** Draw a bar chart to represent the information.

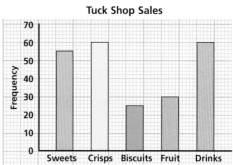

Tuck Shop Sales

b) The same amount was sold of two items. Which two?
   The bars for crisps and drinks are the same height so it must be crisps and drinks.

3 Draw a vertical line graph to represent the information. Don't forget to include a title and label the axes.

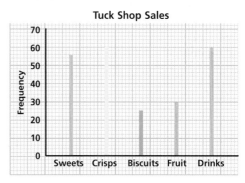

Tuck Shop Sales

? Now try these...

1 A football fan recorded how many goals her team scored in each match she watched.

Goals scored	0	1	2	3	4
Frequency	5	3	4	1	2

a) Draw a pictogram for this frequency table. (You can use one symbol for all the lines. Let ⚽ = one goal.)
b) How many matches did the fan watch in total?
c) Which number of goals was scored least frequently?

2 The results of a survey on pupils' favourite pets are shown in the table below.

Pet	Dog	Cat	Rabbit	Guinea Pig	Fish
Frequency	56	45	28	32	24

a) Illustrate this information by drawing a bar chart.
b) Which pet was the second most popular?
c) How many pupils were asked in total?

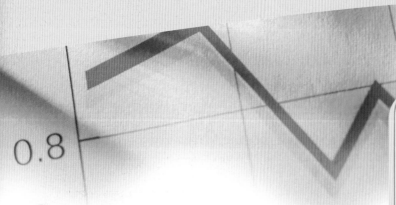

0.8

i You need to know...

- **how to represent grouped data in a frequency diagram**
- **how to construct and interpret simple line graphs.**

Grouped data can be shown in a **frequency diagram**, which is a lot like a bar chart (see p.104). However, for the height of each bar to show the frequency accurately, you must make sure the class intervals are all the same width (see p.103).

The horizontal axis needs to be labelled to show the lowest value and highest value in each class interval and there should be no gaps in between the bars (see Example 1).

Line graphs are normally used to show a pattern of change over a period of time. Each item of data is plotted using a small cross or dot (like when you plot coordinates). The crosses/dots are then joined up using straight lines.

? Now try these...

1 The table to the right shows the number of hours 20 children spent watching television over one weekend. Draw a frequency diagram to show this data.

Hours	Frequency
1-5	5
6-10	8
11-15	3
16-20	3
21-25	1

2 The table to the right shows the number of videos sold by a shop in the past 6 years. Draw a line graph to show this data.

Year	Frequency
1999	8000
2000	9000
2001	9000
2002	8000
2003	5000
2004	3000

Examples

1 The maths test results for a class of 30 students are shown in the table below. Draw a frequency diagram to show this data.

Test Score	Frequency
1-10	2
11-20	4
21-30	4
31-40	11
41-50	8
51-60	1

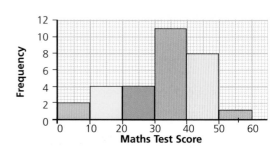

Notice that all the class intervals are the same size. The labels on the horizontal axis come between the bars, rather than under them.

2 The number of rolls of wrapping paper sold by a gift shop each month (to the nearest 100) for a year are shown in the line graph below:

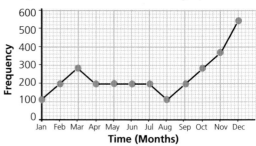

a) During which period were sales constant?
A flat horizontal line means there was no change in frequency, so sales were constant **between April and July**.

b) Between which two months was the largest increase in sales?
A line sloping upwards (left to right) shows an increase and a line sloping downwards shows a decrease. The steepest line is **between November and December**, showing the largest increase.

c) Can you suggest a reason for this increase?
Christmas is in December, which would explain an increase in sales.

Displaying Data

ℹ You need to know...

- **how to construct and interpret frequency diagrams for grouped continuous data.**

Continuous data can be shown in a line graph. e.g. to show the growth of a sunflower (measured in mm) over a period of time. If it is grouped, however, you will need to draw a frequency diagram.

There are two types of frequency diagram. One uses bars to represent the data (see p.104). The other uses bars and lines and is called a **frequency polygon**.

The easiest way to draw a frequency polygon is to start by constructing a frequency diagram using bars, in the same way as shown on the facing page.

You then need to mark the **midpoint** at the top of each bar with a small cross or dot. Finally, join all the points using straight lines.

Alternatively, you can plot the points straight onto the axes without drawing the bars first. Be careful to make sure the points show the correct frequency and are positioned exactly at the halfway point of each class interval.

Example

The heights of 25 children are shown in the table.

Height (cm)	Frequency
120-	6
130-	4
140-	8
150-	7

a) Draw a frequency diagram to show this data.

Remember, the class intervals need to be the same width for your diagram to make sense.

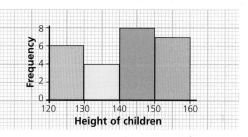

b) Draw a frequency polygon to show this data.

Use your frequency diagram as a starting point. Your crosses/dots must be exactly in the middle of each class interval.

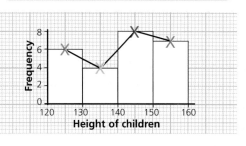

❓ Now try these...

1 The table shows the weights of 25 new members who joined a gym in January.

Weight	Frequency
50<w≤70	5
70<w≤90	8
90<w≤110	7
110<w≤130	4
130<w≤150	1

a) Draw a frequency diagram to show this data.

b) Draw a frequency polygon to show this data.

c) How many new gym members weighed between 90kg and 130kg?

d) How many new gym members weighed under 110kg?

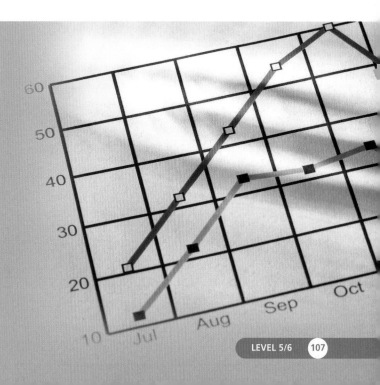

You need to know...

- **how to use bar charts to compare two or more sets of data**
- **how to interpret graphs and diagrams and draw conclusions.**

When two or more sets of data have a connection **comparative** or **compound bar charts** can be drawn so that you can compare and interpret the data.

This graph allows you to compare individual results.

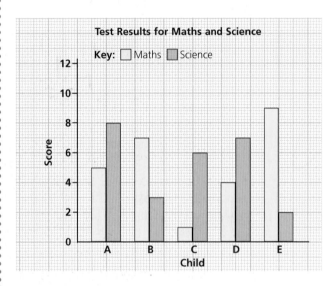

This compound bar chart allows you to compare the totals of both results.

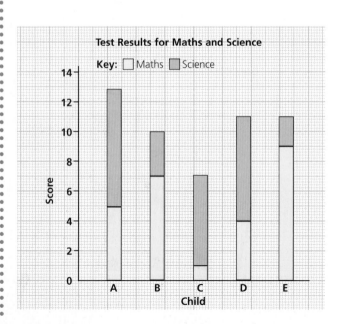

Examples

1 The bar chart shows the number of different coins in Joe's money box.

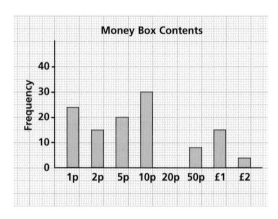

a) Which coin does he have exactly 20 of?

The only bar which shows a frequency of exactly 20 is the 5p column.

b) What is the total value of the 2p coins?

The 2p column reaches halfway between 10 and 20 on the frequency axis giving a frequency of 15.
Total value of 2p coins = 2 x 15 = 30p.

c) How many coins worth less than 5p does he have?

The only coins worth less than 5p are 1p and 2p. From the graph we can see that there are 24 1p coins and 15 2p coins **so the answer is 24 + 15 = 39 coins**.

d) What is the total value of the coins worth 50p or more?

The coins worth 50p or more are:
50p coin with a frequency of 8,
value = 50 x 8 = £4
£1 coin with a frequency of 15,
value = 15 x 1 = £15
£2 coin with a frequency of 4,
value = 2 x 4 = £8.
The total value is 4 + 15 + 8 = £27.

Displaying Data

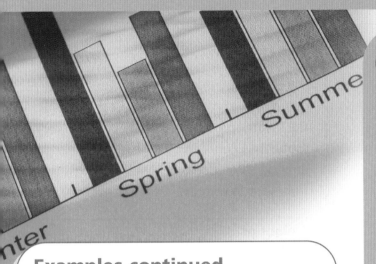

Examples continued

2 The number of people over 17 and the number of people owning a driving licence in a particular street were noted over a period of years. These are shown in the table below.

Year	1970	1975	1980	1985	1990	1995
Over 17	32	27	29	31	33	31
Driving licence	12	17	19	20	24	28

a) Represent this data on a comparative bar chart.

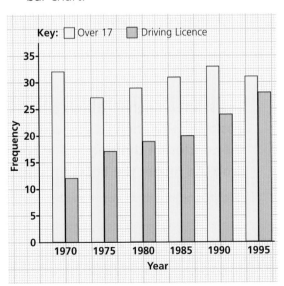

b) Compare and comment on the results.

The graph shows that whilst the number of people over 17 has remained constant over the period the number of people owning a driving licence has increased.

? Now try these...

1 A school is raising money for a new minibus. It needs to raise £15 000. The bar chart shows the amount of money raised.

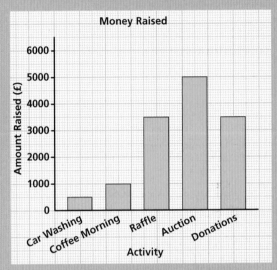

a) How much have they raised so far?

b) Which activities raised the same amount of money?

2 The results of a survey on methods of transport used by students to get to school in summer and winter were displayed in a bar chart.

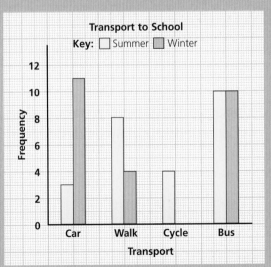

a) How many students took part in the survey?

b) How many students walk to school in summer?

c) Which method of transport was used by the same number of people in the summer and winter?

You need to know...

- **how to draw scatter diagrams and understand correlation.**

A **scatter diagram** is a graph with two sets of data plotted against each other. If there is a relationship between the two sets of data, **correlation** occurs.

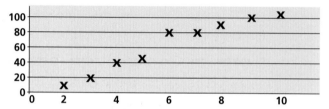

This diagram shows a **positive correlation**. As one variable increases so does the other one.

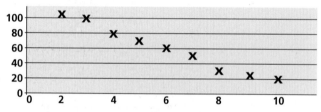

This diagram shows a **negative correlation**. As one variable increases the other one decreases.

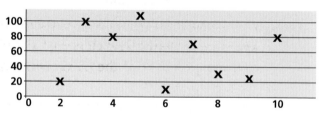

This diagram shows **no correlation**. There is no obvious relationship between the two sets of data.

Example

An experiment was carried out to measure the height to which a rubber ball bounced after being dropped from various heights.

Height of drop (cm)	50	75	100	125	150	175	200
Height of bounce (cm)	20	25	50	60	75	75	100

a) Draw a scatter diagram for the data.
To draw a scatter diagram you plot pairs of numbers onto the graph in the same way as you plot coordinates.

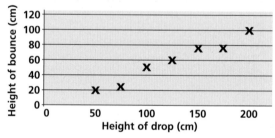

b) Comment on the relationship between the two sets of data.

The scatter diagram shows a strong positive correlation so you can draw the conclusion that the higher the drop the higher the bounce.

Now try these...

1 a) Plot these points on a scatter diagram.

Height (cm)	127	165	149	147	155	161	154	138	145	167
Shoe size	5	8	5	6	5	5	6	4	5	7

b) Is there a correlation? If so, what does it tell us?

2 a) Draw a scatter diagram for the following data.

Distance travelled by a car (km)	50	100	150	200	250	300
Petrol left in tank (p)	55	52	49	43	40	38

b) Is there a correlation? If so, what does it tell us?

Displaying Data

i You need to know...

- **how to draw and interpret data in simple pie charts.**

Pie charts are circular graphs. The circle is divided into sectors and the size of each sector represents the frequency. To draw a pie chart from a table of results you need to work out the angle for each sector. Then you can mark out the angles using a protractor.

Here are the results of a survey of the pets that 24 pupils had. Cat - 6, Rabbit - 4, Bird - 2, Dog - 9, Hamster - 3.

Divide each number by the total number (to find the fraction) and multiply by 360° to find the angle for each sector.

Cat	6	$\frac{6}{24}$ x 360° = 90°
Rabbit	4	$\frac{4}{24}$ x 360° = 60°
Bird	2	$\frac{2}{24}$ x 360° = 30°
Dog	9	$\frac{9}{24}$ x 360° = 135°
Hamster	3	$\frac{3}{24}$ x 360° = 45°

Measure and mark 90° for cat	Measure and mark the angles for rabbit, bird and dog	Check that the remainder (for hamster) is 45°

 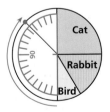 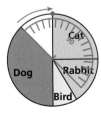

Always use a protractor when measuring angles and make sure you start reading the scale from 0°.

Each sector of the pie chart represents the number of children who have that animal as a pet. For example, you can clearly see that $\frac{1}{4}$ of the pupils have cats and that the most popular pet is a dog.

Example

300 pupils were asked what they do for lunch at school.

a) Copy and complete the table.

School canteen	165	$\frac{165}{300}$ x 360° = 198°
Packed lunch	75	$\frac{75}{300}$ x 360° = 90°
Go home	60	$\frac{60}{300}$ x 360° = 72°

b) Draw a pie chart for this information.

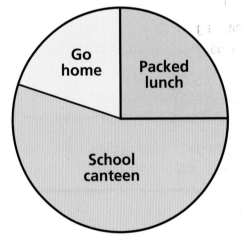

c) What proportion of pupils bring a packed lunch?
The slice for packed lunch is $\frac{1}{4}$ of the pie chart so $\frac{1}{4}$ or 25% of the pupils bring a packed lunch.

? Now try these...

1. Pupils were asked what their favourite snack was. Here are the results: fruit - 15, crisps - 100, chocolate - 165, ice cream - 50, cakes - 70.

   a) Put the information into a table and draw a pie chart.
   b) What was the least popular snack?
   c) What fraction of the pupils chose crisps as their favourite snack?

i You need to know...

- **how to find and use the mode and median of a set of data**
- **how to find and use the range of a set of data.**

An **average** is a value that best represents a set of data.

The **mode** is the value that has the highest frequency. It is the value that occurs most often in the data. The mode does not have to be a number, e.g. it could be the most popular computer game or album in the charts. The mode is a useful average because it is the most common value.

The **median** is the middle value in a set of data, once all the values have been put in numerical order. The median is a useful average because it is not affected by very high or very low values.

The **range** of a set of data is the difference between the biggest value and the smallest value. It is useful because it shows the spread of the data.

If your data consists of numbers you can draw a **stem and leaf diagram** to help you find the mode, median and range.

? Now try these...

1. The number of goals scored by the local football team in their first 11 matches is:
0, 2, 1, 4, 0, 1, 1, 0, 2, 3, 0.
Find...
a) the mode **b)** the median **c)** the range.

2. The attendance register of a class showed the number of pupils present over 15 consecutive days: 26, 29, 28, 29, 28, 28, 29, 27, 30, 29, 22, 30, 27, 30, 26.
Find...
a) the mode **b)** the median **c)** the range.

Example

1. Simon recorded the shoe size of eleven people in his class:
2, 4, 5, 5, 4, 3, 6, 7, 4, 6, 7.

Put the numbers in order first
2, 3, 4, 4, 4, 5, 5, 6, 6, 7, 7

Find...
a) the mode
There are three people with size 4 shoes. This is more than any other so **the mode is 4**.

b) the median
With the numbers in order the middle number (the 6th value) is **5**. **This is the median**.

c) the range.
The range is the difference between the highest size (7) and the lowest (2).
Range = 7 – 2 = 5.

2. Here are the marks a group of nine students got in a spelling test:
24, 13, 26, 25, 24, 24, 30, 19, 17.
Put the data into a stem and leaf diagram and find the mode, median and range.

1	3 9 7
2	4 6 5 4 4
3	0

Think of your place value table. The stem represents the tens and each leaf is a unit.

1	3 7 9
2	4 4 4 5 6
3	0

Rearrange the 'leaves' so that are in ascending order (lowest to highest)

Mode = 24
Median = 24 (5th value counting from top left)
Range = 30 – 13 = 17

Averages

ℹ You need to know...

- **how to find and use the mean of a set of discrete data**
- **how to use the range and one other average to compare two distributions.**

The **mean** is the numerical average. Averages such as a team's goal average in football matches or the batting average in a cricket match are the mean.

The mean is useful because it takes all values into account.

To find the mean of a set of data simply add up all the values and then divide by the total number of values.

$$\text{Mean} = \frac{\text{all the values added together}}{\text{total number of values}}$$

To use the mean and range to compare two sets of data, remember that the mean is the value that best represents the set of data and the range shows the spread of the data – the larger the spread the less reliable the data.

❓ Now try these...

1 Find the mean and range of the following sets of numbers.
  a) 12, 14, 8, 14, 6, 12
  b) 49, 52, 57, 47, 51, 55, 52, 49, 53, 44
  c) £3.20, £3.70, £2.40, £3.50, £2.80
  d) 15°C, 16°C, 22°C, 21°C, 23°C, 17°C

2 These are the means and ranges for the times that it takes two taxi companies to get a taxi to a customer.

	Mean (min)	Range (min)
Super Cabs	9.7	14
Steve's Taxis	9.9	5

You have to leave to catch a train in 20 minutes. Which company would you call? Explain your answer.

Examples

1 The highest temperature (in °C) was recorded each day for a week: 18, 16, 21, 19, 23, 21, 22. Find the mean temperature.

$$\text{Mean} = \frac{18+16+21+19+23+21+22}{7} = 20°C$$

2 Use the data in the table below to find the mean number of sweets per tube.

> To find the mean of a large set of discrete data recorded in a frequency table, you need to add an extra column to the table.

No. of Sweets in a tube	No. of tubes	No. of sweets in a tube x No. of tubes
34	12	34 x 12 = 408
35	24	35 x 24 = 840
36	31	36 x 31 = 1116
37	18	37 x 18 = 666
38	15	38 x 15 = 570
	Total = 100	Total = 3600

$$\text{Mean} = \frac{3600}{100} = 36$$

This is the total number of sweets involved

3 Here are the runs scored by two cricketers in their last 6 innings. Which cricketer would you choose to play on your team? Explain your answer.

George	45	75	38	64	65	43
Ian	90	12	23	81	8	122

First calculate the means and ranges:

George: $\text{Mean} = \frac{330}{6} = 55$

Range = 75 – 38 = 37

Ian: $\text{Mean} = \frac{336}{6} = 56$

Range = 122 – 8 = 114

Ian has the largest mean but he also has the largest range. Choose George because he is more consistent – he is more likely to get his average number of runs. Ian has a chance of getting a high number of runs but this is risky because the large range shows he performs inconsistently.

You need to know...

- **how to use terms associated with probability.**

Probability is all about chance. It involves trying to work out the likelihood of an event happening, e.g. 'Will it rain tomorrow?', 'Will you come top in maths?' To answer probability questions, you need to understand how the following words are used:

impossible, very unlikely, unlikely, equally likely, likely, very likely, certain.

The probability line below shows where each word comes on a scale. Look at the chance of randomly choosing a blue cube out of a bag in each of the given situations:

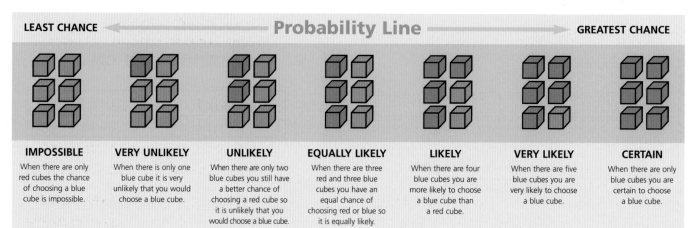

LEAST CHANCE			**Probability Line**			GREATEST CHANCE
IMPOSSIBLE	**VERY UNLIKELY**	**UNLIKELY**	**EQUALLY LIKELY**	**LIKELY**	**VERY LIKELY**	**CERTAIN**
When there are only red cubes the chance of choosing a blue cube is impossible.	When there is only one blue cube it is very unlikely that you would choose a blue cube.	When there are only two blue cubes you still have a better chance of choosing a red cube so it is unlikely that you would choose a blue cube.	When there are three red and three blue cubes you have an equal chance of choosing red or blue so it is equally likely.	When there are four blue cubes you are more likely to choose a blue cube than a red cube.	When there are five blue cubes you are very likely to choose a blue cube.	When there are only blue cubes you are certain to choose a blue cube.

Example

If two dice are thrown and the numbers added together describe the likelihood of the total being...

a) at least 2

The lowest total you can get with two dice is 2, because 1 + 1 = 2. This means that all the totals you can score are at least 2. You are **certain** to score at least 2 with two dice.

b) a total of 11

There are two ways you can score 11 with two dice, (5,6) and (6,5), but there are lots more other scores you could get. You are **unlikely** to score 11.

c) a total of 16.

The highest total possible with two dice is 12, because 6 + 6 = 12. It is **impossible** to score 16 with two dice.

Now try these...

1

Spinner A   Spinner B   Spinner C

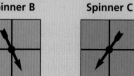

Match the spinners to the following statements:
a) It is impossible to land on red.
b) It is equally likely to land on red or blue.
c) It is certain to land on red.

2 Are these statements true or false?

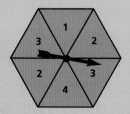

a) There is an equal chance that you will spin a 2 or 3.

b) It is impossible to spin the number 1.

c) It is unlikely that you would spin the number 4.

Probability

ℹ️ You need to know...

- **how to understand and use the probability scale from 0 to 1**
- **how to justify probabilities using either experimental evidence or theoretical probability**
- **that different outcomes may result from repeating the same experiment.**

The probability of an event can be expressed numerically on the probability scale. All probabilities must be between 0 and 1.

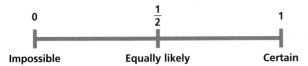

The more likely it is that an event will happen the closer the probability is to 1. The probability of an event happening is usually written as a fraction but it can be written as an equivalent decimal or a percentage (see p.29).

Theoretical probability is based around the idea that events are equally likely to happen if they have the same chance of happening, e.g. heads or tails.

For equally likely events the probability of an event is given using the formula:

$$P(\text{event}) = \frac{\text{Number of favourable outcomes}}{\text{Number of possible outcomes}}$$

In many real-life situations the probabilities are not equally likely and so you need to do a **survey** or an **experiment** to see which option is more likely, e.g. the probability of a car being red can be found by doing a traffic survey. If you repeat a survey it is unlikely that you will get exactly the same result, but the probability fractions should be about the same.

If events are not equally likely and you cannot do a survey or an experiment, then you can look at **statistical data** collected by others, e.g. to find the probability that it will snow on Christmas Day you can look at past records before estimating the probability.

Examples

1 A fair die is thrown. What is the probability of...

a) throwing a six?
Number of sixes on a die = 1.
Total possible outcomes = 6
(The six possible scores are 1, 2, 3, 4, 5, 6)
P(scoring 6) = $\frac{1}{6}$

b) throwing an even number?
Number of even numbers = 3
(The 3 possible even numbers are 2, 4, 6)
P(even number) = $\frac{3}{6}$ = $\frac{1}{2}$

2 A bag contains 2 green counters, 7 red counters and 1 blue counter. Draw an arrow on the scale to represent each probability.

A = Probability of selecting a red counter
B = Probability of selecting a green counter
C = Probability of selecting a blue counter

$P(A) = \frac{7}{10}$ $P(B) = \frac{2}{10}$ $P(C) = \frac{1}{10}$

❓ Now try these...

1 25 discs numbered from 1 to 25 are placed in a bag. One of these is chosen at random. What is the probability that the disc chosen is...
a) a multiple of 3?
b) greater than 15?
c) a prime number?

2 Simon has 10 socks in his drawer, 3 of which are grey. He pulls out a sock at random. What is the probability that the sock Simon pulls out is grey?

3 The National Lottery uses 49 balls numbered 1 to 49. What is the probability that the first ball that comes out is a multiple of 10?

ⓘ You need to know...

- **how to justify probabilities based on equally likely outcomes.**

When there is a number of possible outcomes, if the chance of getting each outcome is the same they are all **equally likely**. If a game is set up so that the different outcomes are equally likely to happen then we say that the game is **fair**.

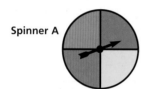 Spinner A   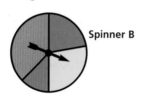 Spinner B

A spinner is to be used to select a colour – red, yellow, green or blue. Although both spinners are made up of four colours, spinner A is divided up equally (fair) but spinner B is divided unequally (not fair).

Tossing a coin has two possible outcomes, heads or tails. On a fair coin the two outcomes have the same chance of occurring, they are not affected by any other factors. They are **equally likely** outcomes.

For many everyday events there are a set of possible **outcomes**, e.g. a football team may win, draw or lose a match. In this case the outcomes are **not equally likely** because they are affected by other factors.

Examples

1 On which colour is the spinner most likely to land? Explain your answer.

The spinner is most likely to land on green because half of the spinner is green and only one quarter is red or blue.

2 A group of four students played a game. Each chose a colour and drew discs from a bag containing 11 blue discs, 3 red discs, 2 green discs and 8 yellow discs. Samantha chose red, Stuart chose blue, Shaila chose yellow and Harjit chose green. The first player to get three discs of their colour is the winner. Explain why the game is unfair.

i) **Harjit can never win because there are only 2 green discs in the bag.**
ii) **There are 11 blue discs in the bag and so Stuart has more chance of choosing his colour.**
iii) **Since there are only three red discs in the bag Samantha does not have a very good chance of getting three discs.**

When you are asked to explain an answer try to give more than one reason.

❓ Now try these...

1 Some marbles are hidden in a bag. The bag is shaken. A marble is pulled out at random.
   a) Which colour marble is most likely to be pulled out?
   b) Explain your answer to **a)**.

2 Here is a square spinner. Decide whether the following statements are true or false.

a) 4 is the most likely score
b) 2 and 4 are equally likely
c) odd and even scores are equally likely
d) a score of 3 or more is as likely as a score of less than 3.

3 Eight cards with the following numbers on are shuffled and a card is picked at random.
   13, 16, 23, 26, 33, 36, 43, 46
   You are equally likely to get an odd number or an even number.
   a) Is this true?
   b) Explain your answer to **a)**.

Probability

You need to know...

- **how to identify all possible outcomes for two or more events and present them in a table**
- **that the total of all the mutually exclusive events is 1 and use this to solve problems.**

For a single event, e.g. rolling a die, you can put all the possible outcomes in a list. For a **combined event**, e.g. rolling two dice and adding their scores, a **sample space diagram** can help to identify every possible result.

Mutually exclusive events are events which cannot happen at the same time. If you toss a coin the event 'obtain a head' and the event 'obtain a tail' are mutually exclusive as you cannot get a head and a tail at the same time.

The **total probability** for all possible outcomes is 1.

P(event will happen) = 1 – P(event will not happen)
P(event will not happen) = 1 – P(event will happen)

If the probability of it raining today is $\frac{3}{10}$, then
P(not raining today) $= 1 - \frac{3}{10} = \frac{7}{10}$.

If you know the probability of an outcome you can use it to solve problems and make predictions (see Example 4).

Examples

1. If you roll a red die and a blue die together how many different ways are there of scoring a total of 7?

   List the outcomes methodically so you do not miss any.

   (1,6) (2,5) (3,4) (4,3) (5,2) (6,1)
   There are 6 ways of scoring 7.

2. a) Draw a sample space diagram to show: the scores of two dice added together.

   First die

	1	2	3	4	5	6
1	2	3	4	5	6	⑦
2	3	4	5	6	⑦	8
3	4	5	6	⑦	8	9
4	5	6	⑦	8	9	10
5	6	⑦	8	9	10	11
6	⑦	8	9	10	11	12

   Second die

   b) What is the total number of possible outcomes?

   There are 36 possible outcomes.

   c) What is the probability of each outcome?
   $\frac{1}{36}$.

   d) Use the diagram to find out the probability of scoring a 7.
   P(scoring 7) $= \frac{6}{36} = \frac{1}{6}$.

3. Out of every 100 people 17 are left-handed. What is the probability that a person chosen at random is...
   a) left-handed?
   P(Left-handed) $= \frac{17}{100}$
   b) right-handed?
   P(Right-handed) = P(Not left-handed)
   P(Not left-handed) $= 1 - \frac{17}{100} = \frac{83}{100}$

4. The probability of passing the driving test at the first attempt is $\frac{2}{3}$. Of 60 people attempting the test for the first time how many would you expect to pass?
   Expected number $= \frac{2}{3} \times 60 = 40$

Now try these...

1. a) Draw a sample space diagram to show all possible outcomes when the score on the two spinners are added together.
   b) What is the total number of possible outcomes?
   c) Find the probability that the total is...
      i) 11   **ii)** 5

2. There is a probability of $\frac{3}{10}$ that a caller will leave a message on a telephone answering machine.
   a) What is the probability that a caller will not leave a message?
   b) Out of 50 callers, how many would you expect to leave a message?

Acknowledgements

The author and publisher would like to thank everyone who has contributed to this book.

All photographic images in this book are © Jupiterimages Corporation.

Every effort has been made to contact the holders of copyright material, but if any have been inadvertently overlooked, the Publishers will be pleased to make the necessary arrangements at the first opportunity.

ISBN: 978-1-905129-40-9

Published by Letts and Lonsdale

Consultant Editor: John Proctor

Contributors: Linda Bakes and Susan Ball

Artwork: Lonsdale and HL Studios

Letts and Lonsdale make every effort to ensure that all paper used in our books is made from wood pulp obtained from sustainable and well-managed forests.